To Aunt R...

89th Birthda...

Best Wishes...

SAPP Y SOORACKS AND BURNT

SUGAR

Sappy Sooracks
and Burnt Sugar

BY

ELLEN ROBERTSON

The Pentland Press
Edinburgh – Cambridge – Durham – USA

Ellen Robertson, 1996

First published in 1996 by
The Pentland Press Ltd
1 Hutton Close,
South Church
Bishop Auckland
Durham

ISBN 1-85821-375-4

Typeset by Carnegie Publishing, 18 Maynard St, Preston
Printed and bound by Antony Rowe Ltd, Chippenham

My Husband,
Alexander, with Love

Contents

Illustrations

Part One
Sappy Sooracks
And
Burnt Sugar

CHAPTER I

Earliest Memories

I WAS BORN ON THE THIRTY-FIRST OF JULY nineteen
hundred and thirty-four at one hundred-and-sixty
Claythorn Street, Glasgow, and when I was one year
old was taken to a children's home. The reason was,
as I discovered in later years, that my mother was a
single parent and lived with my grandfather. He had
persuaded her to have me fostered so that she could,
perhaps, have a better chance in life without the added
worry of me. I have no knowledge of my father—only
that his name was David De Rome. My mother's name
was Jeannie Austin.

From the children's home I was sent to be fostered
by a family who lived in Keith, which is in the north
of Scotland. Being very young at the time, however, I
can't remember them at all. Perhaps it was for the best
because they didn't treat me very well. Once again,
therefore, I was to be returned to the children's home.

Social workers would, as part of their duties, visit the
foster parents every year just to check that the children
in their care were properly looked after. On the day
that I was returning to the children's home they had
to call and check on a lady called Mrs Milne, who was
a widow fostering a boy and girl. As it was quite late
when we arrived, they asked her if she would keep me
overnight. Mrs Milne agreed but felt so sorry for me
that when they came back to fetch me, she decided
there and then to foster me. So at the age of two-and-
a-half I came to stay with my new Mum at Ivy Cottage,

Mum feeding the hens

Enzie Crossroads, near Buckie, Banffshire, where we spoke Buchan; boys were 'loons' and girls were 'quines'.

When I was five years old, Mum enrolled me at Clochan Public Secondary School, which was situated in a small village about two miles away. As there was no transport, all the pupils had to walk to and from school five days a week, spring, summer, autumn and winter in all kinds of weather. Some children had to walk a lot further than the two miles as they lived on isolated farms, but in spite of the distance we travelled, very few of us were late or absent.

Clochan was a typical village school. It comprised an assembly hall, four classrooms, woodwork/cookery room, small staff room, headmaster's study. Both girls' and boys' toilets were outside. We didn't have to wear school uniforms but most of the pupils wore navy or grey. In the winter I wore a navy nap coat of very thick material, a huge woolly scarf wrapped around my neck, across my chest and tied at the back with a safety pin, an astrakhan pixie hat, thick woollen 'itchy' stockings and button boots or wellingtons. I was so 'happit' up that I could hardly move! But when spring arrived, off came the itchy stockings and on went ankle socks, dress and blazer. Sheer bliss! Boys wore short trousers until they were at least thirteen.

We had a headmaster and four permanent teachers, while the music, cookery and gym teachers came once a week. About one hundred pupils attended and most of them came from surrounding villages and farms. We received a good basic education in reading, writing, arithmetic, English, history, geography and science.

Miss Reid was the infant teacher. She was elderly with short cropped grey hair and couldn't pronounce the letter 'R' properly. Miss MacKay taught classes two

3

and three and wore heavy makeup. Mum would say 'I dinna ken fit wye she wears pooder and paint jist tae sit in front o' a puckle bairns.' Miss Paterson, who taught class four and the qualifying class, was a typical school 'ma'am'. She wore a long black dress with a high collar, a cameo brooch, spectacles and kept her hair in a bun. Her first name was Isobel but we called her 'Beldy'. Miss MacClean taught advance classes one and two. She had a mop of flaming red hair and a flaming temper to match.

Our headmaster was Mr Johnstone. He taught advanced three and was married with three children, Robin, Jonathan and Patsy. He always wore a tweed jacket and plus fours. He didn't half shout at us if we did anything wrong! They could even hear him up in the village. His shouting was far worse than getting the belt, although he didn't use the belt too often.

Every week Miss Duncan taught cooking, knitting and sewing. In cookery we made the usual scones, cakes etc. In knitting you started off with a scarf, then socks or gloves, and if you were good enough, you progressed to a jumper. Your first task in sewing was the usual lap bag to keep your knitting in, followed by a cookery apron and then a blouse. As I was staying on for another term, I progressed to making a dress and was allowed to pick my own material. I chose a lovely lemon shade with small white flowers. Miss Duncan was a great teacher and would sometimes take us on picnics in the summer. Mr Wylie was the gym teacher. Every year we had sports and I competed in the one hundred yards and four hundred yards races as well as taking part in the high jump. I would enter for the county sports and won many prizes and points for the school. Although I won all the flat races, I could only manage third place in the high jump. When I was racing, the spectators would shout 'come on the blue' because I always wore blue shorts and a blue blouse. My shorts had a big stain on the bottom where I had sat on some tar. Mum tried everything to get the tar off but it wouldn't budge and as we couldn't afford to buy a new pair, I had to wear them. I was always embarrassed in case anyone would notice the tar stains, so maybe that was why I ran so fast! On one occasion my name and photo appeared in the local paper.

I had numerous friends but some were 'best'. Janet Thompson was a tall thin girl who also lived with foster parents. She always had goodies for her 'play piece' and shared them with me. She also let me have the *Girls Crystal*, which was a magazine similar to the *Bunty*, when she had finished reading it. On occasion during the summer holidays I was allowed a daily visit to Janet. She lived at Farnachty, which was quite a distance from Ivy Cottage, and it took me nearly an hour and a half to walk there. I would leave early in the morning and stay until the evening.

There was an old railway carriage at the bottom of her garden which we called a 'cherabang' (charabanc). Here with some other friends we would play most of the day. Sometimes we would have concerts, but for the most part we would sit around and talk or read. Janet's mum brought us home-made lemonade and biscuits.

Gladys Benzie was small and dumpy. She had two sisters and a brother. Although she was the same age as myself, she acted as though she were older, considering herself worldly wise and acting as though she knew everything. She put vaseline on her eyelashes to make them grow longer and would sometimes be so daring as to put on her sister's lipstick.

Jenny Gordon was goody-two-shoes. She was never ever involved in a row from the teachers or received the 'belt', but she was a 'fine quine' and I liked her. Once there was a Burns night to be held at the school for the local residents. The headmaster wanted volunteers to peel the 'tatties' and 'neeps' for the meal, arranging that afterwards they would go to the Burns Supper. Jenny and I were the only two to volunteer and we soon found out why. There was a one-hundredweight bag of 'tatties' and the same of 'neeps' to be peeled and we only had a small kitchen knife each! It took us hours and by the time we had finished we were too bloomin' tired to go to the Burns Supper.

Jamesina and Freda Phillips were sisters. Freda was quite plump and, with her short brown hair, was rather boyish-looking. Jamesina, on the other hand, was very thin and had white hair and rosy cheeks. They lived on an isolated croft far up among the hills and were full of talk about seeing ghosts. They both had a vivid imagination and scared everybody with their stories. We all thought them rather weird.

Helen Brockie belonged to the Plymouth Brethren and lived with her mum, brother and sister in the nearest village of Broadley. To help finances her mum sold lemonade. Helen became my best friend.

Jessica Yeats wore glasses and had long blonde hair which she wore in pigtails, making her look like Keyhole Kate. She was the school 'bully' and every day threatened to 'get' someone at four o'clock. However, it always fell through because as soon as it was home time, everybody ran like the wind. One day when I walked into the classroom no one spoke to me. At once

I knew why: Jessica had warned them not to speak to me or else! This lasted for two days, after which it was someone else's turn. She did this on a regular basis.

Margaret Stuart had a mass of black curly hair, was always brown as a berry, and was covered in freckles. She was a tinker and belonged to a large family of Stuarts who lived in tents, made clothes pegs and sold them. Most of the family hardly ever washed but Margaret was always clean.

Mary Grant had a lovely singing voice and won many talent contests. She had numerous brothers and sisters and they all lived at Enzie Station House. However, a terrible tragedy occurred, involving this family and another called Farquar. Mary's youngest sister Lola and her friend Gladys went for a secret swim in the burn during the winter. A few days later they both caught double pneumonia and both died. They were only seven years old. Gladys had a twin sister called Cecilia.

I once entered a talent contest myself. It was when I was in Buckie collecting the accumulator for the wireless. A talent contest was being held in the picture hall by a certain Archie McCulloch, who was a talent scout from Glasgow. I thought I would try my singing. I was ushered on to the stage where the man at the piano asked, 'Where's your music, lassie?'

'What music?' I said.

'What key do you sing in then?'

'Key? what key?' (the only key I knew was for the door).

'Right then, what would you like to sing and I'll play the piano?'

'Clementine,' I said.

'In a cavern in a canyon excavating for a mine . . .'

'Next!'

I remember some of the boys too. Donkey Thompson was a tall lanky boy with buck teeth and a high pitched voice. He always joined in the girls' games. David and Alan Clark were brothers. David was the youngest and was quite clever, but Alan was the very opposite. He was the original 'school dunce'. From the time he started school until leaving, he didn't want to learn anything and he always sat at the bottom of every class. The teachers found it impossible to teach him as he was so disinterested in everything, but even so Alan was never late, absent or disruptive.

Andrew Taylor was nicknamed Tiny but grew to be six feet tall. Paddy McPhee once said something cheeky to me so I punched him in the face and broke his glasses. Frank Christie was the best looking boy in the school. Louie, Bertie, Jackie and Maria Capaldi were evacuees and stayed with a local farmer. Although their parents were Italian, they really came from Glasgow.

There were no school dinners as such, but in the winter time, during the war, we were given a huge bowl of home-made soup and a plate of steamed pudding. On the winter mornings too, Helen and I had to make quantities of hot cocoa in the cookery room and take it round in white enamel pails to all the classrooms, giving a cupful to each pupil. If we brought some dry bread or rolls to school, the teachers would spread them for us with a generous helping of lovely home-made jam.

We were also given a small bottle of milk each morning. The bottles were left in crates at the school gate and each pupil took turns to bring them in. A local shopkeeper owned a bulldog called 'Strath' and one morning when it was my turn to bring in the crates I found 'Strath' licking the tops of the milk bottles. You know how bulldogs slaver all the time; it was disgusting. I never told the teachers or any of the pupils, but I never ever took milk at school again!

Every day during the war we carried our gas masks to school. You carried your gas mask over your shoulder in a square cardboard box with a long string attached. We were also issued with identity cards. An air raid shelter had been built at the side of the school and every week we had air raid drill. It was the same as fire drill except that everyone had to put on their gas mask and run into the shelter.

The blackout was strictly enforced and no one was allowed to show any lights after dark. People had to put thick curtains over the windows to ensure this because, when returning from a raid, German planes flew overhead across the North Sea. If they saw any lights they might drop one of their bombs. We recognised the planes by the distinctive drone of their engines.

At that time I was terrified of aeroplanes and had a weird feeling that they were going to fall from the sky straight down on top of me. One morning while I was on my way to school I found that my wellingtons were on the wrong feet, but I was too scared to change them because at the time there was a plane flying overhead. Even now, whenever I hear the sound of light aircraft, I still experience a funny feeling.

One night a farmer named Mr Grant was taking his car from the garage when he accidentally showed the headlights. At that particular time there was a German plane flying overhead and it must have seen the lights shining. It dropped a bomb which landed in a field near the village. There was a terrific explosion, all the houses shook and the windows rattled, and our cottage door and windows were nearly blown out.

Everyone ran outside in a panic but luckily no one was hurt and no great damage had been done except for a huge hole in the field where the bomb had landed. The next day people came from far and wide to see it. That was the one and only bomb dropped near us, though Aberdeen was bombarded regularly on account of the shipyards.

There was also a fleet of both German U-boats and British frigates at the Scapa Flow.

The Gordon Highlanders were stationed at Gordon Castle in Fochabers and the Airforce at Lossiemouth. I would watch the soldiers on their route marches with the pipe band marching in front, and sometimes the army would hold manoeuvres. One day, as I left to go to school, I saw hundreds of soldiers in the fields all around and found that the roads were blocked with army lorries and jeeps. The soldiers were on a training exercise and it looked like a real battle field. Towards the end of the war Polish and German prisoners of war were held in a POW camp at Spey Bay. They worked on the surrounding farms and many of them remained after the war and married local girls.

Chrissie Benzie married a Polish soldier called Jan Piffco and they lived with her parents in a large cottage at Arradoul. There was no electricity in the cottage so Jan built a small windmill in their back garden and transmitted electricity from it into the house. It was a clever idea but as it depended on wind force, sometimes the light would be rather dull, so to make the light brighter he used to place pieces of mirror around the light bulb on the ceiling so as to gain added reflection.

There was one Polish soldier who cycled regularly past our house and whenever he saw me in the garden he would give me a bar of chocolate. He never handed it to me but always left it on the ground and then cycled off. I would have been about eleven then. Mum would often give our own soldiers a cup of tea. When the war ended we had to wear something red white and blue to school. I wore a ribbon.

CHAPTER 2

Ivy Cottage

I LIVED AT IVY COTTAGE, which was a lovely little cottage and at one time had been completely covered with ivy—hence the name. It had a kitchen-cum-living-room and two bedrooms. In the living-room was a black range with a high mantelpiece. The furniture comprised a double bed, two leather armchairs, a kitchen table and four chairs, and a grandfather clock. The wireless stood on a shelf attached to the wall.

The living-room was also equipped with a large cupboard where dishes and food were kept. My bedroom was the smallest room. It had a single bed, small bedside table, huge chest of drawers and a wash stand with ewer and basin. The other room was the 'best' and was kept for visitors. It also had a double bed, a lovely carved dressing table and two fireside chairs and at the window a small round table. There was also a coal fire. The floors were covered with linoleum and rugs and the wall paper had a lovely rose pattern. Every Saturday morning the grate had to be blackleaded, floors were washed and polished, the rugs were taken outside, first bashed against the wall and then thrown over the fence and brushed, and finally the ornamental brass around the mantelpiece was polished until it shone.

Outside there was a front and back garden with a shed, a dry lavatory, and a henhouse. There was no electricity, gas or running water, and an open fire, fuelled by coal or firewood, provided all the cooking and heating. Mum was very elderly (sixty-two) when

Ivy cottage, The porch was added long after we left

she fostered me. The previous boy and girl had been sent to another foster parent because they were being difficult and she couldn't cope with them. Thus it was left to me, at the age of about nine, to help with most of the menial tasks.

One of my chores was to fetch our drinking water from a fresh water spring situated in the middle of a field about half a mile away. I carried the water in two pails on either side of a wooden frame. The frame was placed on top of the pails and I stepped inside. When I lifted them they were evenly balanced and hence much easier to carry.

I had small pails at first but as I grew bigger, so did the pails! This chore had to be done every day and twice on Saturday, as you would never carry water on a Sunday! The buses ran past our cottage every hour and as I got older and became rather self conscious, I used to time my water-carrying so as to perform it between buses.

All the water for washing clothes and personal hygiene was saved from rainwater, which was caught in wooden barrels via the rone pipe. The water travelled along the rone and down the rone pipe into a barrel. A second pipe was inserted at the bottom of the barrel and from this water was diverted into a large zinc bath. Thus we could save quite a lot. On washing day, which was every Monday, the rain water was transferred with pails into a coal-fired boiler inside the shed. When the water was hot, it was transferred again into the wooden tub in which the clothes were scrubbed and washed before being rinsed with more fresh rain water. If it was very warm and sunny, the whites would be spread out on the grass to become whiter. Funny how it never rained on Mondays!

Clothes were ironed with a 'box iron', which was hollow with a flap at the back. This was lifted so as to insert the iron which had a hole at one end in which to put the poker through, by which means it could be lifted into and from the fire. When the iron became red hot it was then lifted with the poker and transferred into the 'box iron'. Another iron was already in the fire in readiness to be switched over when the one in use became cool. Maybe that's where the expression 'too many irons in the fire' came from.

There was no bath or shower in the cottage, so you had to wash in a wooden tub in the shed and the water had to be heated on the coal fire in a large pot or kettle. The dry lavatory was at the bottom of the back garden next to the henhouse. In winter it was freezing.

The hen house had a sloping corrugated tin roof and one day I slid down it and shot off the end, landing with my chin on a barbed wire fence. I had a huge cut underneath my chin. Mum said I was very lucky; it could have been my throat!

Although coal was our main fuel, we had to supplement it with fire wood, which was delivered annually in the form of ten or fifteen medium-sized 'trees'. Mum and I had to saw them into logs, then take an axe and chop the logs first in half, then into four pieces before we could use them for the fire. Some logs were chopped very small to be used for kindling. To achieve this 'operation' we had first to lift the tree on to a wooden stand designed to hold the trunk lengthwise for easier sawing. Mum took one end of the saw while I took the other. It took nearly a month to get this chore completed before the winter came. When I saw the big lorry arriving my heart would sink, as I knew the huge chore which lay ahead.

As we had no electricity in the cottage, our lighting came from paraffin lamps or candles. The paraffin was delivered from the village shop by the grocer's van, which came every Friday. There was also a fish van on Tuesday and the butcher's van on Wednesday.

We were to some extent self-sufficient too, as we kept hens which provided us with white meat and eggs. We grew all our own vegetables, plus fruit such as apples, blackcurrants, rhubarb and damsons. These were stewed, made into jam or eaten as they were. Every week Mum would bake oatcakes and soda scones on a round griddle on the open fire, and sometimes when I came home from school while she was baking oatcakes, Mum would 'accidentally burn' one so that I could have it crumbled in a bowl of cold milk.

The flour and oatmeal had to be collected from the flour mill, which was about two miles away. Milk was delivered from the local farm every morning and we obtained an occasional rabbit from the local poacher. As it was during the war and everything was rationed, we did very well. Sweets were also rationed but sugar burnt with a hot poker gave us candy, and syrup boiled with a little butter gave us toffee. If anyone kept bees during the war, they received extra sugar rations.

Our wireless worked by terminals attached to two batteries, one large dry battery and one accumulator. The accumulator had to be re-charged periodically, so we had two of them. While we used one, I took the spare to be re-charged at an electrical shop in Buckie and collected it the following week. The dry battery lasted for ages but had to be replaced when done.

When I was twelve, together with some other pupils, I went to gather potatoes on the neighbouring farms. We were given an exemption from school for three weeks during the harvest or until the crops were all gathered. We went to various farms and started at seven in the morning, working until four in the afternoon with a tea-break at nine o'clock. Dinner-break was from eleven o'clock until one o'clock, and then we worked until stopping time. We brought our own buckets to put the potatoes in. The field was staked out into patches and each was allocated to two pickers. Next the tractor would come round with the digger to root up the potatoes, which you then gathered in your bucket. When full, this had to be emptied into a cart, after which you hurried back to fill it again until all the potatoes had been lifted. The tractor came back round again and again until the field was cleared. For the first few days everyone's back was aching.

We did not spend more than two or three days at each farm, depending on how large it was. Sometimes six or seven farmers all required our services at once. We were paid seven or ten shillings (old money) per day, depending on how rich or generous the farmer concerned was.

At certain farms the farmer's wife would give us our dinner, which was usually lovely home-made 'tattie soup' and bread-and-butter pudding. Usually we brought our own sandwiches of jam or cheese and we supplemented them with hazel nuts from the nearby trees. Some of the farms had unusual names. Here are a few:

Wellheids, Cuttlebrae, The Core, Howe Core, Scraphard, Slack Heid, Slack End, Tarwathy, Claesterim, Inchholme, Easter Bogs, Wester Bogs, Auchentae, Tulloch Moss.

One memorable day, when I was thirteen years old, drinking water was pumped into the shed. A fresh water spring had been found in our back yard by a water diviner. He had used a long 'Y' shaped branch, walking around the yard until the branch slowly lowered its point towards the ground, thereby indicating where the spring was. After a few days some workmen came and started to dig. They kept on for about three weeks until eventually the spring was found. The well hole was so deep that I was scared to go near it in case I fell in.

Once the water had been found, it was then piped into the shed, where a water pump was attached to the sink. The water was brought up from the well by priming the pump with some water and then pumping the handle furiously. The well water was full of iron ore and at first it was dark brown coloured, though eventually it became clearer. Despite its brownish colour, it was drinkable and, being full of iron, was supposed to be good for you (it made me constipated). Probably today it would be considered a health hazard!

The colour or taste didn't bother me; it meant I had no more drinking water to carry. A really memorable day!

I was clever at school and passed all of the exams. When I was twelve and had passed my Qualifying Exam I wanted to go to Buckie High School and become a teacher. I told Mum and she discussed it with Miss Paterson, but she said that although I had the ability, it would be too expensive for Mum to keep me there as I would have to travel by bus. Furthermore, as I was 'fostered', it wasn't important for me to embark on such a career. This upset me for a long time but I would never have put Mum under any pressure, so I stayed on at Clochan. The school-leaving age was raised from fourteen to fifteen, which meant that I was in the same class for two years.

The school was run very efficiently and was well disciplined. A few of us, myself included, occasionally received the belt. The offences for which it was given were mostly talking or not paying attention and the boys were sometimes given it for having fisticuffs in the playground. On the whole everyone was well behaved and respected the teachers.

I enjoyed the freedom of the countryside and during the summer holidays, after my chores were done, I loved to go barefoot, paddle in the burn, and try to catch fish using a stick, a piece of string and a worm on the end of a bent pin. Alternatively I would catch bees in a jam jar when they landed on the flowers; once I was stung on my face and it was swollen for a week. I wandered for hours in the woods collecting fir cones for the fire or running through the fields picking wild flowers to make into daisy chains. Sometimes I would join my friends and we would either play rounders, go for walks, climb trees, play hide and seek among the 'stooks', or make peashooters and fire rowan berries.

I remember once when I was about seven or eight I climbed on top of a high post and when I attempted to jump down from it my gym slip caught and I was hung up by it. There I was, dangling from the post like a puppet, with my gym slip up to my waist, and my navy blue knickers on show, and nobody around to help me. After 'hanging around' for ages, bawling my head off and nearly hysterical because my gym slip was now around my neck and my vest was showing as well as my knickers, Mrs Grant from the nearby village came along and lifted me down. I was so embarrassed I didn't even thank her. I just fled!

On another occasion, while I was picking raspberries, an ugly, slimy green puddock jumped inside one of my wellingtons giving me such a fright that I fell into a bed of nettles. I was covered from head to toe with blisters and the stinging was almost unbearable. I ran home and Mum soothed them with cold water and some docken leaves. Then she gave me a hot cup of tea, an aspirin and popped me into bed.

I used to go to a farm called 'Tulloch Moss' and was allowed to milk one of the cows called Clover. When you milk any cow you have to remember to press against her side to let her know that you are there. The reason is that they get relaxed and want to sit down.

On one occasion while milking I completely forget to put my head against Clover's side. All of a sudden she began to lean towards me. I screamed, the cow took fright, knocked me over, bolted and nearly caused a stampede. From then on I was very careful. Milk straight from the cow tastes quite pleasant and I always had some after the milking was finished. Before drinking, it was put through a strainer. When a cow had her calf, the first milk she produced was made into a soft cheese. I would be given a slice to eat on the way to school. It was delicious.

Mary and Tibby Stuart were sisters and owned the farm called 'Howe Core'. Mary never combed her hair, while Tibby always wore tackety boots and they both wore sacks tied round their waists as aprons. These were called 'Guano Bags' and a lot of farmers' wives wore them. One day Tibby asked me to bring her a pound of dates from the village shop on my way home from school. When I had bought the dates they looked so nice that I thought I would have just one to taste them. Then I had another one and another one and by the time I arrived home there weren't many dates left.

When I handed Tibby the bag she looked inside and said 'that's nivver a pun' a dates! Are ye' sure ye' ask't for a pun?' 'Of course I did,' said I. 'Richt,' said Tibby, 'I'll see the grocer mysel' on Friday for I'm sure there's nae a pun' o' dates here.' All that week I dreaded Friday coming. You see, she didn't give me the money to buy the dates but put it on her weekly bill, which she paid on Friday! I didn't hear any more about it but they never asked me to buy dates again! I think she knew that I had eaten them.

Sometimes I would go along to the smiddy at the nearby village of Broadley and watch Mr Newlands, the local blacksmith, shoe the Clydesdale horses. It was fascinating to watch. He would take a red hot piece of iron from the fire, shape it on the anvil into a horseshoe, then plunge it into cold water to seal it. He would then remove the old shoe and file the hoof until it was smooth. Another red hot piece of iron in the shape of a horse shoe was pressed into the horse's hoof so that it made a groove for the new shoe to fit. The smoke and the smell of burning hoof was awful. The new shoe was then fitted into the groove and hammered on with nails. I would feel sorry for the horse when the nails were being put in, but the blacksmith assured me that the horse's hoof was so thick that it didn't feel a thing. The blacksmith would sometimes let me work the bellows, which, when pressed, blew air on to the fire to keep it burning.

'Granda Symon' was a bit of a character who lived in Broadley. He was an 'old salt', had a long white beard, owned a parrot called 'Popeye', and knitted all his own socks and guernseys. He had travelled all over the world and would tell us stories of his adventures. 'Fact or fiction', we could never tell, but they kept us fascinated. In his attic he had a large collection of ivory, some sea shells and two huge ostrich eggs.

There was a 'crabbit' old man called Alec Paterson who was nicknamed 'auld pails'. He had just two apple trees in his garden but when the apples were ripe he would stand guard over them until nearly midnight just in case the soldiers who were returning to their barracks might steal them.

On Easter Sunday the fisher folk from Portgordon would come up to the country and go either to the woods or moors to search for sheltered spots where they would make an 'Easter Hoosie'. When they found a suitable place, they would 'claim' it by building a ring of stones in readiness for lighting a fire on Easter Monday when they returned to roll their Easter eggs and have a picnic. This form of 'ritual' was re-enacted every year. We coloured our eggs by boiling them in tea or with the yellow blossom from the broom or whin bushes.

As everything was rationed, there were no chocolate Easter eggs.

In the autumn I picked wild raspberries and brambles for Mum to make home-made jam, and also rose hips which were taken to school and then sent to the hospitals to make rose hip syrup. After the harvest was brought in, the 'Steam Mill' would arrive at the farms and everyone came to help. The sheaves were fed into the threshing mill which separated them into corn, straw and chaff. The corn was caught in sacks, the straw was made into huge stacks and the chaff, which was finer than straw, was used as bedding for the cattle. As I had a chaff mattress on my bed, it was re-filled every year when the threshing mill came. The children were allowed to stand on the stack while it was being built from the bottom all the way to the top. It was great fun but a bit scary as it grew higher and higher. To get off, you slid all the way down.

Once during the harvest I was sent to 'The Core' Farm for binder twine, which is used for tying the sheaves. As I reached the farm and turned the corner towards the barn, I came face to face with a flock of bubbly jocks (turkeys). They are really bad-tempered birds and my sudden appearance must have frightened them because all of a sudden they made a run at me and chased me all through the fields making their horrible gobbling noise. I was so terrified that I jumped the fence and ran like a tornado straight home and straight into the lavatory. I never did get that binder twine!

If I felt hungry or thirsty while playing there were lots of 'wonderful' things to eat. A 'neep' nicked from a farmer's field and smashed into small pieces on the road was a whole meal! Then there was a plant with green flowery leaves and long thick stalks which was crunchy and tasted sweet. I called it myrrh. 'Sappy Sooracks' were small bunches of dark green leaves which grew by the side of ditches, and these were very juicy and tasted sour. Mum said dogs peed on them! There were lots of berries when in season and fresh water from the burn.

Sometimes Mum would allow me to go on the bus to the seaside town of Portgordon, where I would 'wyde' (paddle) in the sea and search for shells or coloured stones on the beach. I had a friend called Eunice Ritchie who lived there. Her father and brother were fishermen and owned a trawler called the 'Jeanie Ann'. Eunice was a great swimmer and swam in the sea but being unable to swim, I was a bit scared of the water. One day during a local holiday weekend we both went to Elgin for the day and hired one of the rowing boats in Cooper Park. We bought our mums a lovely tea tray each, which cost us sixpence in old money!

Buckie had a cinema but I didn't go very often except when there was a Tarzan film showing, which was usually twice a year. Then everybody went.

Once a film called 'The Yearling' came and the whole class went to see it. The headmaster was reading us the story at the time. It was an outstanding film but a bit sad. Then 'The Dolly Sisters', a musical starring Betty Grable and June Haver was to be shown, so I asked Mum if I could go and see it. At first she refused, but after a lot of 'coaxing' she finally agreed, though only on condition that someone would go with me. Accordingly I asked Helen Brockie if she would like to come. She wasn't really allowed to go to the pictures as her family was Plymouth Brethren and disapproved of films,

Playing cricket with Helen Brockie. Myself with bat

but after another lot of 'coaxing' her Mum reluctantly agreed. I felt a bit guilty about asking her to go, but we both enjoyed the film and the bag of chips we bought afterwards. Sheer luxury!

Halloween was a time mainly for making 'neepie lanterns' and false faces. I was allowed to go to a few of the nearby houses, but as it was very dark in the country I would only go out if there was a full moon. When the moon shone it was like being in daylight. Even so, I was too scared to go very far because after all there are ghosts, witches, tattie bogles and whig-maleeries roaming around at Halloween!

The winters could sometimes be very severe and

during one particularly bad one we were completely snowed in. The snow was higher than the cottage and when we opened the door, we had to dig a path before we could get out. The school and the main roads were closed for a week. Although we were stranded, we managed to cope as there was plenty to eat. There was oatmeal to make porridge and we had fresh eggs and chicken. Coal and logs were kept in the shed, so we had heating and eating, but we did have to melt some snow to provide water for cooking and drinking. As soon as the main roads were cleared, I fetched our drinking water from the well, which was completely frozen over. I had to break the ice before I could fill my pails. In severe winter conditions motor cars, buses and lorries had chains on the wheels so that the vehicles could grip the road where it was icy. I thought being snowed in was great fun. I would make slides on the ice and build snowmen and was off school for a whole week!

I loved Christmas. Mum would make a 'clootie' dumpling while I picked sprigs of the greenest holly with the reddest berries to put on top of the picture frames and the grandfather clock. The mantelpiece was reserved for any Christmas cards and I also made some decorations with crepe paper. Mum cooked one of our hens and we had broth, chicken with oatmeal stuffing, and home-grown brussels sprouts and a slice of dumpling sprinkled with sugar. In the evening Mum would make candy and we would listen to Christmas carols on the wireless. For supper we treated ourselves to a cup of 'Camp Coffee' and toast, which was made by sticking a slice of bread on the end of a long, two-pronged fork and holding it in front of the open fire. I once made a Christmas cake at school and some mincemeat pies.

Everyone made a round cake but I chose to make a square one just to be different! As money was quite scarce, we didn't exchange Christmas presents. Mum only had her pension and a small yearly allowance for me, which was really to buy clothes. Mum had arthritis in her hands and couldn't write very well, so when her new pension book came I signed six months in advance! This would not be accepted today.

My clothes were always good quality but bought two sizes too big so that I would grow into them! There were no designer clothes in those days. I did, however, receive two presents at Christmas. Mum had a niece called Bell Brown who lived in Keith and every Christmas she sent me a pair of knitted slippers with a piece of tinsel sewed on the front of them. Sometimes there would be a comic too. Helen Steven, who was Mum's granddaughter and lived in Aberdeen, would send me two or three books on the cinema, which were full of pictures and stories about the film stars. I always looked forward to receiving these presents, especially the books.

I would send for photographs of the current film stars and had signed photos of Bob Hope, Bing Crosby, Dorothy Lamour, Patricia Roc, Margaret O'Brien and Margaret Lockwood, who were some of the famous stars then. I also had a signed photo of Vera Lynn, who was the forces' sweetheart during the war. She signed her photo 'Yours Vera Lynn' as 'Yours' was her hit song at that time.

Mum's family were all married and lived in far-off places, but when they sent their Christmas cards they put some money inside for her. One Christmas she received a cake, which was sealed in a tin, all the way from New Zealand from her son Gordon who lived there. Mum would supplement her pension by selling a few of our hens and some vegetables from the garden to the local butcher. Chickens were hatched every year to keep up our stock. We had about twenty hens and every year Mum had to clip their wings to prevent them from flying over the fence and eating the farmer's newly sown corn.

Whenever Mum killed one of the hens (which was done by pulling its neck) she would hand it to me to hold by the legs. Even though the hen was dead, the wings would continue to flap for ages afterwards. It was something to do with a nerve. Sometimes I would be holding one in each hand and the wings would be flapping furiously which made it pretty scary. Killing poultry and shooting or snaring rabbits was the country way and was accepted.

Mum and I didn't really celebrate Hogmanay, but here is a wee poem she used to tell me:

In the wood. Enzie crossroads, Buckie, about 1939. Mum second from left in the rear group with Auntie Mary behind her. Myself in the centre of the foreground group.

Rise up auld wife and shak' your feathers
Dinna think that we are beggars
We're only bairnies come to play
Rise up and ge'es our Hogmanay
Ma feets cal' ma sheens thin
Ge's a piece an' let me rin

The school was non-denominational; religion wasn't an issue and was confined to Sundays. The Catholics worshipped at St Ninian's Chapel, Protestants at the 'Cock Hat' Kirk and the Plymouth Brethren had an open air service in the Square at Buckie. On Sunday everyone dressed in their 'Sunday best' and walked in the country or visited friends.

Clochan dramatic society met at the school in the winter evenings and I took part in two of their plays. 'Main's Wooing' was one of the plays and together with another five girls and six boys, I was picked to be in a classroom scene. We had to sing 'Ho Ro My Nut Brown Maiden' and the girls danced a polka while holding arched branches covered with flowers. The other play was 'The Wedding' and I played Maude the maid. I wore a long black dress, white apron and a white lace cap and I can still remember my 'lines'. Picture the scene:

Prunella and her mother are in a room and Prunella is crying. I have to bring her a dress so I knock at the door:

Mother – Come in
Maude – Here is Miss Prunella's dress
Mother – Thank you Maude
Maude – What's up?
Mother – Up where?
Maude – I mean is anything the matter?

Mother – No, nothing is the matter.
Maude – Then why is Miss Prunella crying?
Mother – Miss Prunella is not . . . mind your
own business Maude. Go now and
give me the dress!
Exit Maude – I'm sure there's something up!

The Dramatic Society also had country dancing and entered contestants in the local competitions. Once I competed in the Highland Fling and Sword Dance but Olive Fraser, who was an excellent dancer and had won trophies before, came first. I was about fourth but as Mum said, 'it's nae the winnen', Quinie, it's takin' part.'

When I was older I 'acquired' a bicycle. It was not brand new but to me it was sheer magic. Until then I had had to walk everywhere, apart from rare trips on the bus, which cost money. By this time nearly all my school friends had bicycles and we would go for cycle runs after school in the summer evenings. Before I had my own bicycle, I would be given a 'barrie' home by one of the boys. I would sit on the bar of his bike. This was quite common and many of us would get a lift in this way.

I didn't have any toys but I did have some colouring books and pencils and a small teddy bear called Tommy, which had one eye and one arm missing. I loved to read and obtained my books from the school library or from friends. Mrs Henderson, one of our neighbours, gave me *The People's Friend* every week and I couldn't wait to read it. You didn't really need toys in the country; there were so many things to see and do. My imagination was used to the extreme!

We had a grey and white cat called Daisy. She stayed in the shed at night but whenever she decided not to come home, she would scratch on my bedroom window during the night so that I could let her in. I'm sure she stayed away deliberately just to get into my room. Daisy was a good hunter but any field mice she caught were left at the door. We also had a tortoise called 'Sodger Doddy', which hibernated every winter and reappeared in the spring.

Apart from having the measles and a swollen gland, I kept very healthy.

I caught the measles the very day that Mum and I were to go to her son Adam's wedding reception, which was to be held in the Commercial Hotel in Buckie. He had already married in Glasgow but was to have another reception for his friends and relatives who lived up North. I was so disappointed when I couldn't go! Mum had saved a little money and some clothing coupons to buy me a lovely blue silk dress with frilled cap sleeves to wear, but instead I was confined to bed for a week. Mum had decided not to go to the reception but after a lot of persuasion she reluctantly went on her own. However, she did bring me a piece of wedding cake and I was allowed to keep the blue silk dress, which I wore on Sundays.

I had a swollen gland on my neck which developed into a huge abscess. Nurse Middleton, the district nurse, would come in each day to dress it with lint, which helped to draw the poison out. It was extremely painful but she was very gentle and tried not to hurt me. Then, however, she went on holiday and another nurse came, one whom I didn't like the look of from the start. She rode a bicycle with a basket on the front and it reminded me of the woman in the Wizard of Oz who looked like a witch and stole the wee dog. She was rather cruel because although my abscess was very painful, she squeezed it so hard to try and get the poison out that I nearly fainted and she had no sympathy when I cried.

One day when she came I refused to let her touch it and started to run away from her, but she grabbed me, pushed me on top of the kitchen table and held me down. It was sheer agony. I finally managed to struggle free and ran up the garden path in hysterics with blood streaming down my neck. Meanwhile, she just stood there and said to Mum: 'She'll be alright. It's bleeding a lot so the poison must be out.' Mum was furious and refused to let her come back again. Instead she dressed the abscess herself. It eventually healed but has left a scar on my neck.

Baxters' famous factory was in nearby Fochabers, but it wasn't such a big industry then and only made jam. During the school holidays you could obtain work either washing jam jars there or else at Christie's Nurseries, where you would weed the flower beds or hoe the vegetables.

Mum's son 'Dod' (which is Buchan for George) stayed with his wife and family at Orton, near Rothes. As I didn't now have to fetch our drinking water every day, I was allowed to go and stay with them for a week during the summer. At times it could be quite lonely with just Mum and me, and as Dod had a big family of four sons and two daughters who were lots of fun, I enjoyed my 'break'. Even so I was always glad to get back home to Mum again. Betty was the youngest daughter and was the same age as me.

One day while I was there two parcels of venison arrived through the post. Dod's son Jimmy, who worked with the forestry in Inverness, had shot a deer and sent half to his family. As there were no fridges then, the venison had to be cooked right away. It was roasted, stewed, fried, made into rissoles, meat loaves and a few other unrecognised dishes and for a solid week we had venison morning, noon and night. When I went home I was physically sick for days. Mum said that venison was far too strong to have eaten so much and that I could have ended up with antlers!

Dod worked with the horses on the neighbouring farm and he was a bit of a rogue. While he ploughed the fields, he would fill his pockets with corn and as he walked behind the horse and plough, he would scatter it along the furrows to entice grouse and pheasants. Then while they were busy eating the corn, he would catch one of them for dinner. He would also 'collect' some of the hen's eggs from the haystacks before the farmer's wife collected them!

St Mary's Well was at Orton and each year there was a pilgrimage to it. I don't know the history connected with this ritual, only that crowds of religious people came to pray and before leaving they would throw money into the well. After everyone had gone, Dod would fetch a ladle and lift out all the half-crowns before the caretaker came to retrieve the money!

Once Betty and I had a chance to ride on one of the Clydesdale horses. As they have very broad backs and our legs were rather short, we kept sliding down the side of the horse. Betty's dad would shove us back on again but we kept sliding down the other side. It was really funny but a bit frightening, so we had to stop. That was the first and last time I was on horseback. One of her brothers, Johnnie, also worked with the horses and he would groom them every night and polish the bridles until they shone. He won a few prizes for the best groomed horses in the local agricultural shows. Johnnie didn't stay in their house but slept in the cha'mers or bothy. This was a large shed with bunk beds where most of the farm workers stayed. It was the type of building where bothy ballads were sung and composed. Sandy was the youngest. He was learning magic and was quite good. He did the usual card tricks and made a few things disappear.

We would cycle to the old Airforce Base at Spey Bay and visit Betty's married sister. She lived in one of the Nissen Huts which had been used to billet the airmen during the war and had now been abandoned. The huts were made of corrugated iron with just one large room. They had a stove in the middle of the floor with the chimney going up through the ceiling. They were mostly occupied by young married couples or squatters.

CHAPTER 3

Glasgow and Marriage

WHEN I WAS ALMOST FIFTEEN and about to leave school, the authorities decided that Mum, who was now in her seventies, was too old to look after me and that I should be returned to the children's home until I reached sixteen. Both Mum and I were devastated and she pleaded with them to let me stay, but although they were sorry and understood how she felt, those were the rules. Mum didn't want me to go back to the home so after much discussion with her married daughter, who lived in Dalmuir West near Glasgow, it was decided that I should stay with her.

Imagine how I felt! I had come to have a deep love for Mum, Ivy Cottage and all my friends. I so hated the thought of leaving that for weeks I couldn't sleep. I cried all the time and kept asking Mum why they didn't consult me about it and why couldn't I stay and look after her instead. However, the decision had been made and there was no turning back. To make it a bit easier for both of us, Mum decided that she would travel to Glasgow with me for a few days. So after arranging for some of the neighbours to look after everything until she returned, Mum and I boarded the train for the long journey to Glasgow and Dalmuir West. This was in August, 1949.

Although we both had mixed emotions, the journey became quite exciting, for neither Mum nor I had ever been outside Banffshire before. After what seemed like ages, we arrived at Glasgow, where her daughter, whom

I was to call Auntie Mary, met us at the station. We then had to board a tramcar, something which we had never seen before, to where she lived. My first impression was very disappointing. I thought it would be a house like our cottage but instead it was what was called a tenement building. To make things worse, it had two flights of stairs to climb after you were in the building even before going into the house. It made me very claustrophobic.

After two weeks Mum had to go home. It was awful and I cried for ages when she left, because apart from missing her, I knew how she must have felt about going home to a lonely cottage to be on her own. I thought it was so cruel.

When I went up on holiday to see her it became so traumatic that I begged Mum to let me stay. Yet we both knew it would be hopeless. Mum eventually became too old to cope on her own and she had to sell Ivy cottage. She came down to Dalmuir to stay but she didn't like it at all. Mum said that she never saw blue skies any more and felt imprisoned. She couldn't walk out of the house as easily as when staying at Ivy cottage. She was pretty frail and had difficulty in walking, so that she had to use a stick, but in the fine weather I did manage to take her to the park or to sit on the benches in Castle Square, which was just round the corner from us. Mum went back up to Buckie to stay with one of her daughters for a short time, but six months after her return she died at the ripe old age of eighty-four. I was told then that she only came down to Dalmuir because of me! That made me very sad.

After a while I settled down to town life. Auntie Mary, who never had a family of her own, was rather strict and reminded me of a sergeant major, so that I was a bit scared of her. She worked as a bus conductor on the SMT buses and the passengers called her Highland Mary. Even the policemen were glad when she was on back shift, as she kept the rowdies in their place!

My first job was working as a junior in the Scottish Wool and Hosiery Store in Clydebank. It was a very old-fashioned shop with an old-fashioned staff. We sold wool, baby clothes, lyle stockings and interlock knickers with elastic round the legs. They reached down to your knees. Auntie Mary wore these just in case the passengers could see up her skirt when she went upstairs on the bus to collect fares. I didn't think it made the slightest difference.

While serving in the shop, we had to wear dark clothes but, being young, I wanted to wear something more colourful. One day, therefore, I put on a bright yellow dress which I had made at school.

All the customers commented on how fresh it looked and I was quite pleased with myself, but at closing time the supervisor took me aside and said 'I think you should put on something a little more conservative tomorrow.' I didn't stay very long in this job and moved on to Galbraith's Stores, which was a grocer's shop, also in Clydebank. The staff there were around my own age and we wore white overalls. One of the girls who worked there, Edith McGinley, firmly believed in her 'stars'. One Sunday she walked all day in Dalmuir Park in the pouring rain because her horoscope had said that she would meet a tall dark stranger. I think she's still single!

I was allowed out on Tuesdays, Thursdays and Saturdays and would go either to the pictures or to the dances. There were three cinemas in Clydebank and one in Dalmuir, The La Scala, The Bank, The Empire and The Regal. There were four dance halls, The Town Hall, Dalmuir Masonic, Clydebank Masonic (which we called Todds) and the Co-operative Halls in Hume Street. The 'in' dancing then was the quickstep, foxtrot, waltz, tango, square tango and of course jiving. The girls would line up at one end of the dance floor and the boys at the other end and when the dance was announced, the boys came forward to choose a partner. If it was a 'ladies' choice', then the girls chose. On some nights you would have partners all the time but on others you would be a 'wall flower'. However, it didn't matter much as it was usual then for girls to dance together. The dancing cost two shillings and sixpence and your hand was stamped with a rubber stamp to prove that you had paid. In the ladies' room there was a machine which for a sixpence delivered a 'scoosh' of perfume. It was always 'Evening in Paris' or 'Californian Poppy'.

At Dalmuir Park in the summer evenings there was open air dancing, talent contests and bathing beauty competitions. Once one of my friends, who wasn't really a bathing beauty type as she had bandy legs, entered for one of the competitions and came first. On that particular night, however, only two girls entered. During the dark evenings there were illuminations.

The cafes all had 'duke boxes' and for a shilling you could play three records. While listening to your record, you could have a glass of American Cream Soda and the dish of the day, which was hot peas and vinegar.

It was while I was standing in the queue for the dancing at Hume Street that I saw a fellow called Alex with some of his pals. He had jet black wavy hair which was cut in a D.A., wore a drape suit and crêpe sole shoes. I wasn't very impressed with him at first because

Alex

he smoked and was showing off all the time, but after getting to know him he seemed to be all right.

Alex lived with his family at 85 Dornal Avenue, Yoker. He had just been demobbed from the army and was working along with his brother delivering sacks of coal for the Co-operative Coal Merchants. It paid well but this was only temporary until his application came through for a job in the Royal Ordinance Factory, where his father worked.

We would often meet at the dances and after a while he asked me to go the pictures. It was such a romantic film – 'King Kong'!! We soon began dating regularly and eventually on 28 March 1952 we were married. The ceremony took place in the Dalmuir Parish Church with the Minister, Mr Martin, presiding. For a short time we lived with Alex's parents. This wasn't very convenient either for his family or for ourselves, so after about three months we bought a room and kitchen with an inside toilet for two hundred pounds at No. 17 Dunn Street, Dalmuir West.

After buying the house money was pretty scarce, and only the kitchen was furnished. Mum had left me a small sum of money from the sale of Ivy cottage so we bought some second-hand furniture and a gramophone. One Sunday we had gone up to the Barra's and had seen one for sale at seven and sixpence. It was the kind you wound up with a handle and played large 78 records, which were made of wax. These could be melted down and made into flower pots. They were very 'trendy'.

One day something went wrong with the gram-ophone and Alex decided to try and fix it. He took off the turntable but at that point the huge spring that you wound up with the handle suddenly uncoiled and flew

Courting

out of the gramophone with such force that it spun around the room rebounding off the four walls. We had to keep ducking in case it hit us. The spring wouldn't go back in again, so that was the end of the gramophone.

Working on the coal lorry was very hard work. Alex and his brother had to carry hundredweight sacks of coal on their backs and shoulders, sometimes up four flights of stairs and about twenty times a day.

Winter was the worst time. Then the bags of coal would freeze solid and cut his hands when he was lifting them and of course when it rained it was thoroughly miserable. He would come home absolutely filthy and so black with coal dust that all you could see would be the whites of his eyes. Although we had an inside toilet, there was no bath or shower, so he had to bathe in a zinc bath filled with hot water to wash all the coal dust off, and I had to scrub his back! During the time when he was working on the coal lorry, I was expecting my first baby and I was worried that it would be born looking like the 'golly on the jar'! Although he had left the army, Alex joined the Territorials and in addition to training once a week at their headquarters, he also went for two weeks every year to various Army camps. As he was in the Highland Light Infantry, he wore a McKenzie tartan kilt and white spats and was one of the smartest soldiers in the 'Terries'. Princess Margaret was the Colonel-in-Chief at the time and when she came to visit the regiment, Alex was chosen to be in the Guard of Honour. He was in the Territorials for nearly ten years.

We had marvellous neighbours in Dunn Street. They were all young married couples and some already had children or, like me, were expecting their first baby.

The tenement had three flights of stairs with three houses on each landing, two of which had inside toilets. The other toilet was on the landing. There was a communal drying green at the back. As no one had washing machines then, you either hand-washed everything or used the 'Steamie'.

Anne Robertson Shirkie was born at Braehome hospital in Helensburgh on 12 October and – hooray hooray – didn't look like the 'golly on the jar'. We called her after Mum, whose maiden name was Jessie Anne Robertson, but we dropped the first name. Money was still short and for something to put in her bootee for her first Christmas we could only afford to buy a little wooden doll which cost a shilling. We had been married almost a year when Alex got started in the ROF, working shifts as a maintenance engineer. After that things got much better. We stayed in Dunn Street for twelve years before moving to the Faifley, and had another daughter, Linda, as well as two sons, Billy and Melvin.

Part Two
Cookie Shines
And
Carry Outs

CHAPTER 4

Making a Start at Beatties' Biscuit Factory

O PPOSITE OUR TENEMENT BUILDING in Dalmuir there was a broad pavement and every day stretching along it would be a row of babies in their prams. It was quite safe to leave them there and housework could be done while keeping an eye on them from the window. When the babies got older and were sitting up in their prams, anyone passing by would stop and talk to them and sometimes give them a biscuit or a piece of chocolate, and if any of them were crying the passer-by would 'shoogle' the pram until they fell asleep.

We lived near Dalmuir Park, which had swings, maypole and a sandpit. There was also a duckpond, fountain and a burn where the children caught 'baggy minnows'. Most of the mums took their children to the park regularly and while the children played they would sit knitting or chatting.

When Anne was three, Linda two and Billy just one year old, we went for a short holiday to Prestwick. We rented one room, with the use of kitchen facilities. It had been advertised in the paper. As we didn't have a car, Uncle Adam drove us there and back. The weather was sunny and as the kids were young we didn't need much spending money. They were quite happy with a pail and spade, a paddle in the sea and an ice cream cone. We went back again the following year.

Once we went to Burntisland. Our upstairs neighbour

Anne, Billy and Linda at Prestwick Beach, 1957

told us that a friend of hers had a holiday chalet there and that we could rent it for the fair fortnight. Once again Uncle Adam drove us there. The 'chalet' turned out to be a wooden hut with a tin roof. There were two beds, a small cooker and a rickety table and chairs. The water for cooking and drinking was fetched from a pump in the middle of the site and there were communal washrooms and toilets. The hut was situated beside a cemetery and a railway. Whenever a train passed, we thought it was coming right through the middle of the hut and the rain rattled off the tin roof.

Burntisland itself was a small market town with shops, a play park and a boating pond with rowing boats for hire. The hut was, to say the least, pretty uncomfortable, so for most of the time we stayed out. By going underneath the railway bridge at the camp site, you

Melvin at one year old, 1960

could reach the beach. It was covered with huge jelly fish and we had to be careful not to get stung. We walked along the beach to Kinghorn but on the way back a sandstorm blew up. The sand was driving against our bare legs and it was so painful that the kids were screaming.

Some distance from the shore stood a huge rock and when the tide was out you could walk to it, so one evening after tea we all set off for the rock. We got there all right but on the way back the tide began to come in again so fast that we had to run like the wind. Even so, before we reached the beach the sea was up to our ankles. By this time the kids were cold and frightened, so when we got back to the hut I bathed their feet in hot water and mustard, gave them their supper and tucked them up in bed. By morning they were fine. I was relieved when Uncle Adam came to take us home!

'Did you enjoy your holiday?' asked Uncle Adam.

'Don't ask!'

I enrolled Anne and Linda in Betty Stuart's dancing classes at Agamemnon Street, Dalmuir. They were taught ballet and tap and appeared in the dancing displays at the Lyric Theatre in Glasgow. Anne had the lead in two of the dance sequences. She danced and sang 'Glow little Glow-worm' and also danced and sang 'A Tisket a Tasket'. Linda was in 'Wee Willie Winkie'. (Well she was just wee!) The dance costumes became increasingly expensive to buy and as I was expecting Melvin at the time, the girls had to end their dancing 'careers'. However, I don't think they were too bothered.

The children went to Dalmuir Primary School. Anne and Linda joined the Brownies and then the Girl Guides. Billy and Melvin joined the Shipmates and then the Boys' Brigade. When we moved to Craig Park Street in the Faifley they went to Edinbarnet School. About this time their dad bought a Lambretta scooter for travelling to work.

After we had moved to the Faifley, Babcocks and Wilcox, who had taken over from the ROF, banned all overtime. There were rumours that the factory was soon to be closed and the workers to be made redundant. Anne was now twelve, Linda eleven, Billy nine and Melvin five and had started school. So to help out financially, I took a 'temporary' job on the 'twilight shift' in Beatties' Biscuit Factory. The 'twilight' was an evening shift which ran from five o'clock in the evening until ten o'clock on Monday to Thursday and from four o'clock until nine o'clock on Friday. This was a good shift for many families as mothers were at home during the day and fathers in the evening. My 'temporary' job was to last ten years!

Beatties' Factory was situated near Drumchapel and made plain, cream and chocolate biscuits. They were mainly produced for Marks and Spencers' home and export markets. The first night I started at the factory was a nightmare. The heat, which was coming from the ovens, added to the noise from the dough cutters, was quite terrifying and the sweet smell of biscuits was so nauseating that I nearly walked back out again. However, as there were another four girls starting too, I didn't. To make matters worse we had each been issued with thick white cotton crossover overalls and white turbans and I was wearing a thick woollen polo neck. I was practically fainting!

There were six large 'plants', each with a huge oven and long conveyor belts on which the biscuits, when baked, came along in rows and had to be lifted off and packed into trays or boxes. They had to be lifted quickly before they fell off the end of the belt and into the 'shan' tray. For weeks I had nightmares about the biscuits falling off the end before I could catch them! At the bottom of the belts were small conveyors with spaces which were called flights. These held a certain amount of biscuits for packaging, which were put through the wrapping machine and then on to a shute. The packets were then weighed, checked for loose seals, packed into cartons which were sealed with strong tape, and then lifted on to pallets. These were then transferred, by means of an electric jack, to the store room. Shan trays caught any biscuits that were misshapen, broken or burnt.

Each carton held forty-eight half-pound packets or thirty-two one-pound packets, depending on which were required, and the pallets held approximately sixty to forty cartons. On most nights we produced eight to ten pallets.

On each 'plant' we were allocated a specific job. Here is an example of how one of the plants was operated. Six or seven girls lifted the biscuits from the conveyor belt and filled the flights, another girl operated the wrapping machine, another two weighed, two checked and packed and another two sealed the cartons before lifting them on to wooden pallets, which were then transported to the store room by another two girls operating the electric jack.

Although this was one typical night's work, each plant produced different types of biscuits and therefore operated differently. For instance, there were the creaming and chocolate plants. It really didn't matter which specific job you were allocated, it was constant team work and really hard going. The shortbread plant was the worst, as the shortbread fingers had to be lifted straight from the belt and into the packets before being sent down the conveyor to be put through a crimping machine and then packed. There must have been thousands of shortbread biscuits hurtling down the belt and as they came down haphazardly, some of us had to form them into piles of eight fingers so that they could more easily be lifted into the bags. About thirty girls were needed to operate this plant and by the time we were finished, our backs were aching and we had 'lift yer biscuits' ringing in our ears!

We were allowed a twenty-minute tea break and later on a ten-minute smoke or toilet break; if there was time, perhaps we would be allowed a 'quickie'. During the 'quickie' break the chargehand would shout, 'Watch yer bloody time and mind it's a "dout" no' a fag!' meaning that we weren't to smoke a whole cigarette! The conveyor belt didn't stop for the breaks as the factory worked on a bonus scheme, so that the more you produced the more you earned.

Some of us worked as 'spares' and took the places of the girls who were going for their break to ensure that the work was continuous. My basic wage at that time was two pounds ten shillings, but with bonus I could earn five pounds. Most of those on the twilight shift were women, but men operated the ovens and two male mechanics maintained the wrapping machines.

Everyone wore white cotton wraps over overalls and white turbans except the chargehands and supervisors, who wore blue. There was an undercharge and charge-hand on each plant and two supervisors who alternated between day shift and twilight shift.

I travelled from the Faifley to Beatties' with six other girls in 'Dan's Van', or sometimes travelled on the bus to Clydebank and walked along Drumry Road. Dan lived in the Faifley and as he didn't work, he used the van to take us to and from Beatties'. We each paid a shilling there and a shilling back every day, but we didn't pay for the journey back until he came for us. The reason was that sometimes he got drunk and didn't turn up, so that we had to walk home. Working in the factory was quite an experience but the girls were nice to work with. Some were 'rough diamonds' and others, like myself, were pretty naive. Language? Well, that was something else! Sometimes funny, sometimes vulgar. Working on the belts was constant and conversation was limited but straight to the point, and not always directed to anyone in particular.

'Hey girls, we're honoured tonight. We've got "Mrs Hat" and Yogi on the belt.'

Barbara, or 'Mrs Hat' as she was nicknamed, lived in the 'Mansions' at Anniesland Cross and always wore a fancy hat when travelling to work, as she didn't want her neighbours to know that she worked in the evenings, especially in a factory. May was nicknamed 'Yogi' because she was very health conscious and ate lots of yoghurt. She too didn't want her friends or neighbours to know that she worked in Beatties'. May told us that if there were visitors when she got home from work, she would sneak into the bedroom, slip into a little black number, and say that she had been to night school.

'Hey, May,' said Sadie, 'whit did ye dae at night school?'

'I went to art classes for painting.'

'Wis that paintin' hooses or paintin' by numbers?'

'Did ye practice on yersel' first?' shouted Nellie.

May wore heavy eye shadow and lipstick but she had a good sense of humour and took all their jibes in fun. She told me that before coming to work in the factory she was under the impression that everybody sat at long tables and packed biscuits into boxes while listening to the 'tranny'. She explained that whenever she passed the factory she could see the girls sitting at tables and had thought that they were packing biscuits, never realising that it was the canteen and that they were having their tea break. Like myself, May had rather a shock when she saw the 'real' factory. Naive? There were no 'sitting-down' jobs.

Gena worked on the creaming belt and Grace, who was the undercharge, took a dislike to her. Every night she would keep yelling at her to 'lift yer biscuits'. After a few weeks of this harassment, Gena lost her temper, lifted a full carton of biscuits, threw them at Grace, knocking her over and shouted 'lift the bloody biscuits yoursel'. Then she walked out.

'Hey, Mary, whit's wrong with you the night? Did somebody steal yer scone?'

'No I just don't know if I should have stayed at hame and finish ma bloody fight wi' "him" or come tae ma bloody work!'

'Hey, you!' Sadie shouts across the belt to Peggy, 'I've a bloody bone tae pick wi' you.'

'Oh aye, what hiv' a bloody done noo?'

'Well you've just went an' telt yer man how much money we earn in here an' he went an' telt my man an' noo my man's cut my bloody wages! That's whit ye've bloody done!'

After that Sadie never spoke to Peggy for months.

'Here comes "Sam the Bam". That man never bloody smiles!'

'Sam the Bam' was one of the oven men and very rarely smiled. Whenever I passed him I always said 'hello Sam' until one night he said, 'By the way, hen, ma name's no' Sam its Tommy.' I didn't know that 'Sam the Bam' was his nickname! (Naive?)

'Nellie, did you get a Valentine the day?' asked Betty.

'A Valentine?' shouted Nellie, 'A ★★★★ Valentine! a'm bloody lucky if a get ma ★★★★★ wages!'

Nellie came from Drumchapel and was a real 'rough diamond'. She was subject to withdrawal symptoms if she didn't get her 'carry out'. On one occasion she had a fight with her husband and came in with a cracker of a black eye. Everybody was being very sympathetic towards her but, 'Don't worry aboot it, girls,' she said, 'this is nothin!' I've only got one bloody black eye but that b★★★★ got two!'

Now 'carry outs' were packets of biscuits that some of the girls took home 'illegally', and some looked on it as part of their bonus. This was the norm although most of the girls, myself included, were too scared to try it. The packets were hidden in different places throughout the factory during tea or toilet breaks and after work was finished the girls would sneak off to get them. There were many different ways in which these biscuits left the factory. Lap-bags tied round the waist were hidden under the girls' overalls and then filled with packets. Others wore elastic garters, each of which could hold four packets, two at the front of their legs and two at the back. Thus eight packets could be taken out. Sadie had done this one night, but as she was clocking out two packets started to slide down her stockings. She just managed to reach the cloakroom before getting caught.

One girl wasn't so lucky. One of the supervisors saw her taking her 'carry out', followed her into the cloakroom and confronted her, and she was immediately dismissed. Nellie wore an old girdle so that she was surrounded with packets! On one occasion she thought she would be smart and put a huge bar of chocolate in her girdle. However, it started to melt and she had to rush to the toilet and get rid of it. Some tucked the packets inside their bras or stuffed their pockets.

One supervisor knew about such 'carry outs' but turned a blind eye. 'They think I'm daft and don't know they're takin' biscuits,' she said, 'but I can hear the bloody packets rustlin' and they're walkin' up the passage like bloody crinoline ladies.'

'Wasn't that a shame about Margaret McPhee getting her books for comin' in drunk?' said Anne. 'And tae think "Boozie Bobby" stotts aff the rubber doors at the creamin' belt nearly every bloody night and gets away wi' it. Its no' bloody fair.'

Margaret McPhee fed the dough into the ovens and also kept an eye on the stacker in case any 'shan' biscuits got through and went on the conveyor belt. She was a very quiet girl and never said anything out of place to anyone. Then on Friday afternoon she was celebrating her fortieth birthday and came to work drunk. One of the oven men reported her to the supervisor, but when Margaret saw her she started swearing and shouting and told the supervisor exactly what she thought about her. She was dismissed on the spot. Margaret had worked in the factory for ten years and had never caused any trouble before.

It was a regular habit for a few of the girls to come in a bit tipsy on a Friday, but because they worked on the belts we could see which girls were tipsy and cover up for them by sending them on the first tea break to sober up with coffee before they were discovered. Unfortunately Margaret worked at the other end of the factory, so we didn't know about it.

'Hey, Sandra, is it true that Sheena's got anither fancy man?'

'Aye, Sadie, it's true. She's been married three bloody times and this is her third fancy man. I don't know how she finds the bloody time!'

Sheena was a big blonde girl who worked on the 'transport' and operated the jack. She had indeed been married three times. Her first marriage hadn't worked out and had ended in divorce. Her second husband was killed in an accident. A few years later she married his friend. Sheena did have several 'fancy' men too.

'Hey, girls,' said Sadie, 'wid ye like tae sign this "get well" card for Cathy Sinclair. The poor lassie's had a hell of a time and she's back in the Western to have one of her legs amputated.'

'Of course we will,' said Nellie, 'whit a bloody shame! We'll hae a whip roon as well for some flowers.'

Cathy Sinclair was a lovely person. She was married with a young family and lived in the Faifley. She travelled to work with me in Dan's van. Cathy was troubled with very bad circulation and sometimes could hardly walk because her toes were so painful. To ease the pain, the doctor had eventually to remove her toe nails. This helped for a short while until the circulation in one of her legs got so bad and painful that the only solution was to amputate. Within a short time both legs were amputated from the hip. Cathy's courage was unbelievable. She had a small invalid car and travelled all over the place. However, her condition worsened and she died a few years later.

'Hey, girls, here come the "Dolly Sisters".'

'They're mair like bloody Fran an' Anna.'

Rita and Peggy, two of the cleaners, were nicknamed the 'dolly sisters' because they went everywhere in the factory together – even to the toilet.

They would both go into the same cubicle and as they also carried their mops and pails it would be quite a struggle for them both to get in. It was hilarious just watching them, and we wondered how they managed to negotiate once inside, but they did. There was nothing 'weird' about them; it was just their way. Peggy would joke that perhaps Beatties' would give her a gold watch when she retired. Peggy didn't get her gold watch but the girls did present her with a pair of 'gold' wellingtons which they had painted.

'Oh no!' shouted Betty, 'I've got a bloody skelf in ma finger an if I hiv' to go tae "Hi Jeannie" tae get it oot, I'll need stitches when she's finished. She's blind as a bloody bat!'

'Maybe she'll just dab it with witch hazel instead!'

Jean or 'Hi Jeannie' (hygiene), as she was called, was the first aid lady for the factory. She wore thick glasses and even with them was a bit short sighted. We all dreaded going to her, especially with a skelf, as she could hardly see your finger! Nancy had to go once and nearly fainted. Anything other than a skelf was treated with an aspirin or a dab of witch hazel.

'Do you think we'll go on strike girls?' said Nellie, 'I heard from "Sam the Bam" that because of this heat wave it's too hot in the factory for the day shift to work so they're thinking about striking. Come to think about it, it's too bloody hot in here every night. The heat builds up before we bloody come in.'

'Ella,' I said, 'if we go on strike, can I borrow your "bivvy" tent to take the kids to Prestwick for the weekend? We have one but could use another.'

'Aye, nae bother, hen, come up and get it after work.'

Early Holidays

W E DID GO ON STRIKE. It was in the summer during the sixties when there was a tremendous heatwave and the factory was stifling because of the additional heat from the ovens. As I didn't have to go to work on the Friday night, Alex and I decided that we would all go camping for the weekend with our two small 'bivvies'.

We arrived at Monkton, near Prestwick, where the camp and caravan site was, and it was quite empty except for a few residential caravans. We booked in and the attendant told us to pick any place we liked, so we chose a lovely grassy spot right in the middle of the site. We unpacked and put up the tents, which were only three or four feet high, then went off to the beach.

When we came back later we could hardly see our tents because the site was completely filled with huge continental tents and caravans. Our little bivvies were right smack in the middle of them all! It was so embarrassing; our tents were so small that we couldn't even stand up in them. To make matters worse, the camp site was next to Prestwick airport and about three in the morning the jets and jumbos would fly over the site. I'm sure that they were no more than inches above us. The noise was deafening!

The next morning we got up before anyone else, washed in the communal washrooms, and headed for the beach, where we stayed until late before returning to our tents. Just as well the weather was good!

'Ellen how was your camping weekend?' asked Ella.
'Don't ask!'
'Hey, Nellie, whit are ye givin' up for Lent?'
'Swearin'.'
'Swearin'? whit aboot stoppin' yer cairry oot?'
'Whit! stop ma "cairry oot" and give me bloody
withdrawal symptoms? Nae bloody likely.'

Every year when Lent came around, some of the girls
were adamant about giving up swearing, smoking and
eating sweets etc. However not one of them ever gave
up taking their 'cairry oots', which I thought defeated
the purpose of their sacrifices!

'Does anybody want tae join the money "minoge"
or the premium bond "minoge"? asked Babs, 'Ye can
have a "turn" in baith if ye like.'

Babs ran both menages and they were on a twenty-
week basis. In the money menage each person paid one
pound for twenty weeks and took 'turns'. However, if
it was the first turn, you seemed to be paying a pound
forever and if it was the last one you thought your turn
was never coming.

The premium bond system was similar but you paid
two and sixpence per week and received a Premium
Bond at the end. It was quite a good way to save and
years later one of my Premium Bonds was a winner
and I received one hundred pounds.

'Right,' said the chargehand, 'May and Ellen, you
two go to the tin wash tonight.'

'Oh no!' we both groaned, 'not the tin wash!'

The 'tin wash', as is obvious, was where the biscuit tins were washed, and it was the only non-bonus
job in the factory. The tins were put into a huge steam
machine and after the washing and drying process was
finished, they came hurtling down a metal conveyor

grid. Can you imagine the noise it made when hundreds of tins rattled along the metal grid? It was horrendous. We then had to lift the tins off the grid and stack them on to trolleys. By the end of the night we were practically deaf!

'I went to the doctor today, girls,' said Nan, 'and guess what? I'm bloody pregnant.'

'Do you want our congratulations or condolences then?'

'Make it condolences, because at bloody forty I didn't want another wean, and besides being pregnant at my bloody age, things could go wrong.' We all had a 'whip roon' for Nan and bought her a lovely lemon dressing gown and slippers to match. Nothing went wrong at the birth and Nan had a beautiful daughter. She named her baby June.

I once worked with a girl on the 'creaming' who had a baby boy when she was forty but had no loving feelings for him. She told me that her husband had to change and feed the baby and her two older children helped too. I thought it was very sad and felt sorry for her and the baby. She left soon afterwards and I hoped as time went by that she would learn to love the little fellow.

'Hey, Sadie, are ye' goin' any holidays this year?'

'I'm going "doon the watter" to Rothsey.'

'I once went a sail "doon the watter" on the banana boat,' said Pat. 'I know its the sludge boat but its spotless inside and we got a nice cup o' tea.'

'Are you goin' on holiday at the fair, Ellen?'

'Yes, we're going camping.'

'What, bloody campin' again? Did ye no' have enough the last time?'

By now we had a better car and a continental tent,

so we went on another camping holiday but this time ventured a bit further afield. We went as far as Dornach! Our car was a two-door Morris Minor so we all set off, Alex, myself, the four kids, our luggage, pots and pans in the car and the camping gear on the roof rack! The car was struggling a bit, especially when we came to a steep hill, and we all had to get out to let Alex drive the car up the hill. It was quite a good camp site and the weather was scorching. I had to do the cooking outside on a small primus stove and the tent was boiling hot during the day and freezing cold during the night. We didn't have sleeping bags! One day when we went into town I found that I had left a packet of butter on the folding table which was leaning against the side of the tent. With the weather being so hot, the butter melted and when we came back there was a huge greasy stain all the way down the side of our brand new tent. The air was blue!

We moved down to Cullen for the last few days. The day we were leaving, Billy decided to go fishing but promised he would be back in plenty of time before we left. We dismantled the tent, put it on the roof rack, packed everything else into the car but Billy still hadn't appeared. We waited and waited and then started to worry lest something might have happened. So we put the tent back up again, unpacked the rest of the gear and were just about to go and look for him when he sauntered round the corner. The air was blue! (again)

'Hey, Ellen, did you enjoy your camping holiday then?'

'Don't ask!'

'Hey, girls,' said Rose, '"Sam the Bam" told me there's a time an' motion man coming to the extension to time how many more packets of assorted biscuits we can pack. That's all we bloody need and they'll likely time Nancy as she's the fastest packer.'

The 'extension' was part of the factory where plain, chocolate and cream assorted biscuits were packed into bags from cartons of previously baked biscuits which had been stored. These biscuits were also used for the Christmas tins. The number of bags that each girl had to fill was quite high. If one-pound bags of assorted biscuits were required, each girl had to fill two hundred and sixty bags, and if it was three-quarter bags of cream biscuits, three hundred and forty had to be filled. That was before you made any bonus. So it wasn't surprising that we were 'annoyed' about being timed again. Nancy was picked and she filled ten more than the original number and more than the girl who was being timed on the dayshift.

'Who the ***** on the back shift filled the bloody extra bags?' shouted on of the girls from the day shift.

'I ***** did,' said Nancy, 'Do you want to dae somethin' aboot it then?'

For a while Nancy wasn't very popular with either the 'twilight' or the day shift.

'It's Fair Friday next week, girls,' said Nellie, 'We'll have to get ready for the "cookie shine".'

'Cookie shines' were small parties held at the Fair and at Christmas, usually in the toilets during the tea and toilet breaks. Gin, whisky or vodka – even 'coffee' was smuggled into the factory in vacuum flasks as well as cakes, sandwiches and sweets in shopping bags. Instead of going to the canteen for your tea break, you went to the toilets. Not the cubicles, I hasten to add, but the area outwith, which had a few seats. There the goodies were shared out while a few songs would be sung and a few jokes told. Nellie had a deep singing voice and always rendered 'The Old Rugged Cross'; Babs gave us 'The Wee Cock Sparra' and – wait for it – I sang my party piece, 'Evening Shadows'. This was all in the space of fifteen to twenty minutes! As our breaks were arranged in relays, the 'cookie shines' lasted until work finished, and no one was outrageous.

CHAPTER 6

First Promotion

Hey, ellen, Betty Chalmers the supervisor wants to see you.'

'You wanted to see me, Mrs Chalmers?'

'Yes, we're looking for another undercharge for the "belts" and as you're a good worker and have never been off, we're giving you the job. You can collect your yellow turban on Monday.'

'What did Betty Chalmers want?'

'I've just been made an undercharge.'

'Whit?'

That's exactly how it happened. She didn't even ask me if I wanted to be an undercharge. The undercharges wore yellow turbans and their job was to make sure that once the chargehands had allocated the number of girls to each 'plant', they kept running smoothly.

As I was used to taking orders, not giving them, I found it difficult to have to place the girls on specific jobs. However, they were all good workers and didn't give me any trouble apart from the clearing up after work. After the plants were shut down, we had to sweep all the floors, clean the wrapping machines and tidy up in general, especially if Marks and Spencers were coming to inspect the factory.

Now this was the time when the 'carry outs' were picked up. As a result there was a shortage of 'after work cleaners'. Those who didn't take any biscuits were left to tidy up, which, as you might guess, didn't please them. I solved the problem by becoming a little bit 'tactful'.

'Right, girls, I need four volunteers, you, you, you and you!'

'Christ, she's got her "I'm in charge" bunnet on!'

This worked, and I was careful to pick different 'volunteers' each time so that everyone had a fair go. Undercharges were really glorified workers and helped with the tea and toilet breaks. If one of the girls working on your belt was required on a busier one, or if there was a shortage of labour, you took their place at the belt for the whole shift, so really you worked as hard as the rest of the girls. The only good point was a slight rise in your wages, and your bonus was guaranteed provided the girls made any.

'Hey, girls,' said Sadie, 'I've just heard they're startin' a nightshift for men.'

'For men,' shouted Nellie, 'whit dae men know aboot packin' bloody biscuits?'

As there was a big demand for Marks and Spencers' plain and chocolate digestive biscuits, they doubled their order and for this reason Beatties' had to start a night-shift. Although only two 'plants' used to produce these plain biscuits, they were two of the largest and busiest in the factory.

Thousands of biscuits were channelled down these conveyor belts and while some of the biscuits were wrapped, others were being lifted from the belt and put on trays to cool before being taken to another plant to be covered with chocolate. Because of the night shift starting at ten o'clock, we had to work on the belts until the men took over from us. It would have been too time-consuming to switch off and re-start the ovens.

'Oh no! Another three pallets o' biscuits to bloody open,' shouted Anna, 'it's no' bloody fair.'

After the biscuits had been wrapped, each packet had to be weighed and if there were any light ones, they were re-opened and put through the flights again. When the nightshift took over, the men got rid of the scales and packed straight off the shute into the cartons without weighing or checking for unsealed packets. As a result, when Teresa, who was on the quality control, opened a carton and discovered a light or unsealed packet the whole pallet of cartons had to be checked. Guess who had the 'pleasure' of opening the cartons – the 'twilight' shift of course. The nightshift didn't get off with this for very long, and were warned to do the job properly.

'Another year, another fair, another "cookie shine".'

'Are you goin' on holiday this year, Nellie?'

'Holiday? if I get anither black eye, my holiday will be visitin' him in bloody Barlinnie!'

Our car and caravan

'Where are you going for your holidays, Ella?'

'I'm goin' to Ireland, hen.'

'Ireland!' Babs shouted, 'Ye better take yer bloody steel helmet an' flack jacket.'

'Are you goin' away this year, hen?' Ella asked me.

'Yes, we're taking the caravan to Blackpool.'

'That's handy,' said Nellie, 'if you run oot o' money you can always use the caravan for tellin' fortunes.'

'Aye an' ye can wear yer turban!'

We now had a new car (Hillman Minx) and a small four-berth caravan, so we decided to try Blackpool. Driving along the motorway, we were all singing 'The Wild Rovers' at the top of our voices when we noticed people waving and pointing at the car. At first we thought they were waving at us so we waved back. Then the car started to shudder so we pulled over and discovered that the caravan had a puncture. We had been singing too loudly to hear the blow-out. We seemed to be miles from anywhere except for a pig farm, which looked deserted. Alex struggled to get the wheel off and after what seemed like ages the farmer and his son came to help. They helped him to remove the wheel and as it was Sunday and all the small garages were closed, they drove Alex to one on the motorway which was open, got the repair done, drove him back and helped to fix the wheel back on again. We were so grateful but the farmer wouldn't accept any payment. They were true 'Good Samaritans'.

We travelled on again until, going over the Shap right on a bend, we had another puncture. This time it was the car but we had a spare wheel, so between dodging the cars that were coming round the bend, Alex finally managed to fix it. We eventually arrived at Freckleton caravan site, which was not far from Blackpool, where we had another two punctures. That made four in all! Nevertheless the kids enjoyed the beach, donkey rides and the amusements, and the weather was sunny. At night the caravan was a bit cramped when all the beds were down, and I felt claustrophobic. On the way home and coming back over the Shap one of the wheel trims flew off and rolled down the embankment. We didn't stop to retrieve it!

'Did you enjoy your holiday, hen?' asked Ella.

'Don't ask!'

Some of the factory girls had other skills but found it difficult to find hours that suited them elsewhere. Jean worked at the creaming and was also a dressmaker. Irene, who worked in the extension, was a hairdresser, while Sheena baked lovely wedding and birthday cakes (ingredients 'compliments' of Beatties). Sadie and Agnes were on the chocolate belt and both had certificates for typing.

'Hey, Ellen, I hear your man got a job as a Jannie.'

'Yes, at Milngavie Primary. We're flitting on Monday.'

'Milngavie? Is that where the snobs come from?'

'Will ye' start wearin' a fancy hat to work then?'

'I thought Jannies were old. Well, the Jannie at my school was.'

After being a Supernumerary Janitor at different schools in the area, Alex gained a permanent position at Milngavie Primary School. It was an old school built in 1875 and had coal boilers. Although the school was in Hillhead Street, the janitor's house was at South View, which was down the hill from the school next to the station. The house was one part of a row of terraced houses which were nearly all vacated as they were to be demolished to make way for a car park. We were very private there, with a secluded lawn at the front. Here at the weekends, and weather permitting, we had all our meals out of doors and as we were near the station, I could now travel by train to Drumry and then cross the Boulevarde to the factory. Alex picked me up at night with the car. By this time Anne and Linda were working in the main branch of the Clydesdale Bank in Glasgow, Billy was at Douglas Academy and Melvin at Milngavie Primary.

About three years later we moved to Hillhead Street, which was just across the road and up the school brae from where we stayed. We were allocated the headmaster's house as it was no longer compulsory for headmasters to occupy tied houses.

The house, which had eight rooms, was nearly as big as the school. There was a large back and front garden and the house was separated from the school by a high wall, which gave us privacy. There was a beautiful staircase in the house with two landings and a lovely stained glass window. Two of the front rooms, which were partitioned off from the rest of the house, were used by the school for lessons.

'Keep your backs straight, girls, and don't slouch.'

'Who the ★★★★★ that shoutin'.'

'That's Betty Settle, she was in the ATS during the war and still thinks she's in the bloody army.'

Miss Settle was the 'Head Bummer' of dayshift and supervised the supervisors. She had been in the forces and held herself very erect. She reprimanded the dayshift girls so often for slouching that every time they saw her they would automatically straighten up! Her sister Ruby was a chargehand on dayshift and also ran the 'in' shop, which opened on a Thursday and sold Beatties' own biscuits at cost price.

'Hey, Ellen, was that an Alsatian I saw in your car the other night?'

'No,' shouts Pat, 'that wis her man!'

'Yes it was an Alsatian. It's Alex's brother's dog, but he's got problems keeping it and wants to know if we'll have it. I don't want a bloomin' dog – never mind an Alsatian, but we've agreed to keep it for a few days until he can arrange something.' But a few days turned into a few years.

Kintra, as she was named, was a beautiful light-coloured Alsatian and after a couple of days she settled in without any fuss and I was persuaded (reluctantly) to keep her. Her kennel name was Kintra of Alnyn and she had a pedigree. What Uncle Willie didn't tell us was that she was pregnant, and one day, out of the blue and behind the settee, she gave birth to five jet black Labrador pups.

Linda was on holiday from work at the time and we both went into a panic as we saw Kintra constantly lifting the pups with her mouth. We thought she was going to eat them! We sent for the vet and after he had calmed both us and the dog down, he explained that she was only trying to lift them and hide them somewhere else. The vet took four of the pups but left us with one for Kintra's sake. The puppy was gorgeous and we called him 'Scooby Doo'.

We kept 'Scooby' for three months and as it was impossible to keep him permanently, we had to find a good home for him. A lady who worked beside Anne took him and when he left we were all in tears. For six years Kintra was part of the family but when she got older, she had to have an operation and failed to survive. We were heartbroken. Kintra was buried at the bottom of the garden.

'Hey, Ellen, Betty Chalmers wants to see you.'

'You wanted to see me, Mrs Chalmers?'

'Yes. Margaret Kerr, the "blue coat", is retiring, so we're putting you in charge of the extension. You can collect your blue overall on Monday.'

'Whit did Betty Chalmers want?'

'I've just been made a chargehand.'

'Whit?'

Once again that's exactly how it happened. She didn't even ask me if I wanted to be a chargehand. On Monday evening I collected my blue overall and white turban with a blue edge. The chargehands didn't share the cloakroom or toilets with the girls but had a room within the factory which was a bit more 'up market'. We had our own toilets, wash hand basins and 'easy' chairs. There were five chargehands: Betty, Violet, Agnes, Big Jenny and myself. The chargehand duties were basically the same as those of an undercharge, except for filling in the girls' time and bonus sheets for whatever belt you were in charge of.

Taking tea or toilet breaks was perhaps voluntary rather than compulsory. Your wages were somewhat higher and received a set percentage of bonus. In addition you could join the pension scheme.

I was in charge of thirty girls in the extension. My undercharge was Bessie Naismith and my machine operator was Jean Cassidy. As the girls worked with the 'finished' biscuits, they could also be sent to work on the belts when needed. We called ourselves the 'reserves'. There was a long narrow conveyor belt the full length of the extension and along each side, fitted to benches, were iron brackets. These were upright and were designed to hold eight cartons of assorted biscuits. There were twelve of these on each side of the conveyor. On the bench in front of the large brackets was placed a small bracket into which a designed 'shape' was fitted to hold the amount of biscuits required for each individual packet. Depending on the size of the packets required, these 'shapes' could be removed and replaced with others. The girls stood in front of the 'sets' and, taking the biscuits from the various cartons, placed them in the 'shape'. Then they slipped the cellophane bag over the top and slid the biscuits into the bag. The packets were then placed on the conveyor, sealed with the crimping machine, and packed into the cartons. Whenever assorted packets were required, each girl had at least three hundred individual bags to fill each night.

All of the empty bags had to be counted by hand before giving them to the girls to fill. Sometimes the 'sets' would be full, which meant that twenty-four bundles of three hundred bags had to be counted. I suggested to the supervisor that if you counted the first three hundred bags and then weighed them, you could save all the rest of the counting by weighing the remainder in bundles. She replied that that would not be possible because some of the empty bags might be a bit 'thicker' than the rest. I wonder who was really 'thick'; bags were made of only very thin cellophane!

In the extension, apart from packing assorted packets and Christmas tins, we also had to operate a wrapping machine which had small flights. These flights held four custard cream biscuits, which were wrapped in cellophane. One hundred of these small packets were packed into each carton and then exported to Saudi Arabia. The machine itself was called the 'four machine' or 'Genevieve', because it was so old.

'Hey, Ellen, I hear that one of your lassies is getting married.'

'That's right, Sadie. Anne's been engaged now for two years so they've decided to get married.'

'We better bung up the bonus then, girls,' said Nellie.

'Aye, yer bloody right. Weddings are expensive,' said Babs. 'It cost me a bloody fortune when my daughter got mairrit.'

'Hiv' they got a hoose?'

'Yes, they've got a flat in Strathblane Road in Milngavie.'

'They're quite right tae get a hoose. It's nae bloody use stayin' wi' you,' said Sadie, 'I done it and we did nothing but bloody fight!'

'Thanks for the invitation, hen,' said Ella, 'I'm lookin' forward to it. When's the "bottlin" hen?'

'On Sunday, Ella.'

The 'bottlin', or show of presents, was as usual held on the Sunday and was nearly a disaster. Anne's friends were to come in the afternoon and my friends and a few girls from the factory in the evening. According to tradition, the men were to disappear and leave the women to have their party. Thus I was left to distribute the whisky etc. I wasn't sure how much to pour in the glasses, so whenever there was an empty glass I kept filling it up to the top, with the result that whereas Anne's friends had a whale of a time, by the time my friends came there was no whisky left, and as it was Sunday we couldn't buy any.

I was so embarrassed, but everyone else thought it was hilarious. However, my luck was in because, as per usual, some of the girls from the factory had a wee 'hauf' bottle in their handbags. So with drinks all round, a sing-song and plenty of food, it wasn't such a disaster after all.

'Whit did Alex say aboot runnin' oot o' drink, hen?'
'Don't ask!'

Anne and Robert got married in June and the wedding went thoroughly well. It was held in Milngavie Town Hall and Strachan Kerr were the caterers. Months before the wedding, we bought a couple of bottles of whisky each week so that the guests didn't have to buy their drinks. The band was The Jackie Currie folk group (Jackie's sons are now the famous Currie Brothers) and everyone had a lovely time. Three years later Linda and Derek were married in May and had the same kind of wedding. They went to live in Helensburgh.

'That wis a great weddin', hen,' said Ella. 'I've still got my "hauf" bottle in my bag.'

Although I had made a lot of friends in the factory, we didn't really socialise as everybody had their housework, shopping and dinners to organise during the day. However, Bessie Naismith came through to visit occasionally and would stay for tea, and then we would travel to work together. Bessie loved coming to Milngavie as it was so different from Drumchapel and she would pretend that she was on holiday for the day. Sadly, years later Bessie's kitchen caught fire and she was trapped behind the door and didn't survive.

'Sadie, are ye goin' away for September weekend, hen?'

'Aye, Ella, I'm goin' a bus run to Blackpool to see the illuminations.'

'Are you goin' away, Ella?'

'No, hen. It's my son's twenty-first birthday and I'm givin' him twenty-one pounds and that's a lot o' money.'

'Ellen, hen, are you goin' away for the weekend?'

'Yes, Ella, we're thinking about going to Aviemore.'

We now had a bigger car and caravan and we also had a Marine Ply sailing dinghy called 'Brer Rabbit', with oars and a huge white sail on which was depicted a black teddy bear. That September weekend Anne, Robert, Linda, Derek, Billy, Melvin, Alex, myself and Kintra the dog took the caravan and tents and, with the dinghy on the roofrack, we all went to Aviemore. On the way up to Loch Morlich, the road had passing places and an oncoming car was too far over on our side, forcing us off the road and into a ditch. We all had to get out and pull the car free. Luckily no one was hurt. After reaching the loch, we set up the dinghy and the four boys went sailing. Kintra watched them sail nearly to the middle of the loch and then decided to join them. She rushed into the water, jumped on board, and nearly capsized the boat! In the evening the family went to the sports complex for ice skating and we took the dog for a walk. Kintra didn't like the caravan, so she shivered and whined the whole bloomin' night!

'How did you enjoy your weekend at Aviemore, hen?'

'Don't ask!'

'Hey, girls, Yogi's workin' on the transport an' she'll no' bloody like that; it's too much like hard work.'

'I saw her man last night and he looks just like Norman Wisdom but a bit bigger.'

'I went in tae the local shop for my fags,' said Bessie, 'and they had bloody Marks and Spencers' biscuits on their shelves. I had tae tell them tae get rid o' them before they got the bloody jail. Some stupid idiot in here has been sellin' their "cairry oot" tae the shop.'

'See that wee blonde that works on the creamin?' Well she's havin' an affair wi' one o' the oven men.

When her man's on nightshift, she hands him her keys tae let himsel' in.'

'Betty, I hear that yer man's got a job with the Bearsden Burgh. Are ye movin' there?'

'Aye, we're gettin' a hoose in Courthill, but I don't think I'll like it. I like Drumchapel. I've got a lot o' pals there.'

'Christ,' said Pat, 'I wish I could shift tae Bearsden.'

Betty, or Bearsden Bella, as the girls called her, was allocated a lovely house in Courthill right beside the bus terminus. Her husband was quite happy in his work but Betty complained so much that they had to move back to Drumchapel. She just couldn't cope outwith her environment.

'Whit are ye doin' this weekend Nellie?' asked Pat.

'I'm goin' doon tae the pub for a wee hauf and a sing-song.'

'Whit aboot you, May?'

'We are having friends over for dinner and I've bought a little black number to wear.'

'Oh, a little black number. Is it a wake yer havin' then?'

'Are you doin' anything this weekend, Ellen?'

'We're going to the Partick Thistle "player of the year" presentation dinner dance at the Ellan Gowan Lodge.'

'Christ, did ye hear that girls? Hey, May, that beats havin' friends for dinner.'

'Hey, Ellen, are ye buyin' a little black number?'

'No, I can't afford a new dress, I'm just going to wear the one I had last year and the year before. It's an evening dress, so I don't wear it very often. Anyway nobody is going to notice me as Alan Rough and his glamorous wife Michele will be there. They'll be looking at her.'

'Did you hear that, "Yogi"? That definitely beats having friends for dinner.'

For a few years Alex was the treasurer of the Milngavie Partick Thistle Supporters Club. Every year they held a dinner dance in the Ellan Gowan Lodge for the player of the year. This time it was Alan Hanson, and I was asked to present him with the award. It was interesting to meet the players, their wives and girlfriends. There was always a lovely meal and the dance was great as I had a chance to dance with some of the celebrities.

'Hey, Rose, is yer daughter still livin' abroad?'

'Yes, she's in Israel, workin' in a Kibbutz.'

'Whit the hell's a kiboots?'

'I think it's a communal place where everybody shares the different types o' work.'

'Christ, she could've got a job in here; this is like a bloody kiboots. Sometimes I think they've put the wrong sign up ootside. It should have been "The Loony Bin" instead o' Beatties'. You have tae be half daft tae work in here!'

'Aye, ye're right, Mary. If you threw a bolt anywhere in here you're sure tae hit a bloody nut.'

'Pat, have the polis stopped arrestin' yer brother yet?' asked Isobel.

'No, they lifted him again last night. Somebody saw him on the bus and told the polis. My mother's nearly havin' a nervous breakdown.'

'Well, I don't think he looks anything like "Bible John",' said Isobel. 'I wish they'd catch the bugger an' let me go back tae the dancin'.'

Three girls had been murdered while coming home from one of the dance halls in Glasgow and the police were looking for a suspect who was called 'Bible John'. Many people thought Pat's brother fitted the description and he was reported frequently to the police. Although he had been cleared of all suspicion, they had to arrest him each time it was reported.

One Sunday morning while we were living at South View, detectives came to our door and asked if we knew who had lived in the house next to ours. They wanted to question them in connection with 'Bible John'. We didn't know who had lived there as the house had been empty when we came to stay, but one of the other neighbours told them that the people who had lived there were now in South Africa. For some time after that we felt somewhat uneasy. 'Bible John' has still not been caught!

Another year, another Christmas, another 'cookie shine'!

CHAPTER 7

Changes in Work

THE BONUS SYSTEM AT THE FACTORY HAD STOPPED and as the girls now received a decent wage, they began slacking in their work. Although the same production was required, we didn't have the same team work on the belts, which made the work rather a strain. I had been ten years on the 'twilight shift' and by now I was getting rather tired and weary of the factory. I thought I could do better than pack biscuits, so I enquired about vacancies for clerical work in the offices during the daytime. About three months later they offered me part-time in the mornings.

'Hey, Ellen, we heard you were goin' tae work in the offices, hen. Is that right?'

'Yes I am, Ella. I've served my time so they're letting me out on parole!'

'Quite bloody right! I wish I had thought aboot it years ago,' said Nellie. 'Working on the backshift just became a bloody habit.'

'You're right, Nellie. I started for Christmas, then I thought I'll just stay to the fair, then I'll just stay to Christmas again, then the fair. It just went on and on!'

'We're goin' tae miss ye, hen,' said Ella, 'ye were the best bloody "blue coat" we ever had.'

'Thanks, Ella. I'm going to miss everybody too. You have all been great to work with.'

I had mixed emotions about leaving. Ten years seemed a long time to be in close contact with the other girls but it had been a 'wonderful experience'.

The scroll which the girls at Beatties'
presented to me on leaving

When I left, they had the usual 'whip round' and presented me with a 'leaving scroll' signed by the girls and a beautiful gold watch.

At first I disliked the office; it was too quiet after the hustle and bustle of the factory and I had to sit at a desk all the time. My duties were to check the invoices and total them up, and as I was used to working quickly, I would have them checked in record time and then sit bored for the rest of the morning. The girls were typical office workers and a few of them thought they were a cut above the factory girls, but I soon put them right on that score.

One day at lunch in the canteen I was talking to Marion, who was leaving to go back to college. I asked casually what her job in the office entailed. She said that she was a stock and order control clerkess and that I should apply for the job; it was full time and rather more interesting than checking invoices. I didn't really want full time and wasn't sure if I would be capable of doing the work, but after a lot of persuasion I decided to 'have a go' and put in an application form. I then had second thoughts and withdrew it. Mr Garret, who was the personnel officer, asked me why I had withdrawn my application. I told him that I thought I might have 'bitten off more than I could chew'. He advised me to leave my application; I could sit with Marion to learn the work before she left, and I would have a three-month trial. I got the job.

I was now working on my own and my duties were to order all the materials for the factory and offices, including all the ingredients for the biscuits, all the cartons, tape, tins etc., and also the medical supplies. I had first to telephone the orders, then confirm by letter, and keep a record of all the stock. I eventually adjusted to office work and made friends with most of the girls. Jean Cassidy also 'escaped' from the factory and came to work in the office. After I had spent four years in the office, the factory closed and we were made redundant. Mr Willis, who was the manager, gave me a good reference for my next employment, which was at Yarrow Shipbuilders.

Before I started working in Yarrow's, I had joined the 'Rand Agency' in Sauchiehall Street in Glasgow. These agencies are used by firms who require assistance for short periods. The girl at the agency asked me if I had ever dealt with wages. I replied that the only time I was involved in such work was in paying out the redundancy payments to the factory workers while I was in the office. 'Oh well,' she said, 'you have some experience. Bowaters in Milngavie are looking for a wages clerkess for a few months until their computer system is set up. Could you start this afternoon.'

There were three of us in the office and I was the only 'temp'. The Kalamazoo system was used for the wages, which meant that everything was done by hand. Every wage slip had to be written out in triplicate and insurance, tax and rebates calculated mentally as you went along. If anyone had their tax code changed and they were entitled to a rebate, this had to be calculated too. Not only did we write the pay slips for Bowaters in Milngavie, but we also dealt with those for the Whitinch branch, and their pay slips had to be finished by Thursday in readiness for the nightshift workers.

By the time the pay slips were completed, Securicor had delivered the money to make up the wages. We were then locked in the office and thousands of pounds was dumped in the middle of the table to be counted and confirmed, so as to ensure that the right amount had been delivered before the Securicor left. We then made up the wage packets. The exact amount of money was always delivered, but sometimes when all the wage packets were filled, there might be some money left over. Then we had to check all the packets again until we found the one that was short. After the wages were completed, we next had to take them to the factory and hand them out to the workers. When Monday came around, you started all over again. Teabreaks were taken at your desk. A lady came round the offices with a tea trolley and as she stopped to speak to everybody on the way, by the time she got round to us the tea was always cold. I was seven months at Bowaters, and was heartily glad when their computer was installed! The agency then sent me to Yarrows on a 'temporary' basis which lasted for 16 years!

I worked at Yarrow Shipbuilders as a clerkess in the Quality Assurance Department. My duties included photocopying, filing, and operating the reprographic machine, which transferred microfilm and microfiche drawings on to paper for easier handling by the engineers. I was also the 'Chief Goffer' (go for this and go for that). The test engineers who worked in the Quality Assurance had their own specific skilled jobs. They tested the propulsion, electrical appliances, engines, galleys, sewage, etc., and these had all to be passed before any ship could be made seaworthy.

There were also field engineers who travelled to various firms and tested any equipment which Yarrow Shipbuilders had ordered before they considered buying. When the galley trials were in progress and the fridges were being tested, I had a chance to sample the ice cream and if the ovens were being tested it would be roast potatoes. During the laundry trials the engineers had their overalls washed.

Mr Fleming, the Chief Dockside Test Engineer, was the boss and was a little 'eccentric'. When he had a headache he sent me to the chemist for Beecham powders and gave me an empty packet to take in case I got the wrong ones. He left pencils on my desk for sharpening and he was such an old fuss pot that I had to make sure the points were sharp enough. He went to the mixed sauna baths every Thursday and would leave early. One Thursday he had just left when his wife phoned to speak to him. I said he had gone to the sauna. When the men heard that I had told her where he was, there was an uproar. They said that she probably didn't know he went to the sauna. I dreaded going to work the next day in case there was trouble, but luckily for me there wasn't. Anyway, he shouldn't have been at the sauna if his wife didn't know!

Mr Fleming also objected to any of the men whistling in the office. He invited Margaret and Sheila, who were the typists, and myself for our Christmas lunch at the 'Dumbuck', but the hotel kitchen went on fire and we were forced to stand outside until it was under control. He was such a snob that because Sheila wore a fur coast, he insisted that she sat in the front of the car beside him!

One of the ship staff was called Tom Jones. Whenever he phoned the office and the men knew it was he, I had to cover the mouth piece, because they would start to sing 'Delilah'. One of the ship managers was called Les Cheffings and when he phoned they would shout, 'Loose chippings on the phone.'

The ship staff invited Alex and me to one of their social evenings, which were held in the Naval building.

When we arrived, the room was full and everyone was milling around, so we headed for an empty table in the corner. We sat on our own for ages until Lynn, who worked in the print room, came over and said, 'I know your table's reserved but can I sit for a few minutes to change my shoes.' We hadn't noticed the reserved sign on the table and feeling extremely embarrassed, made a sharp exit. Alex had worn a black blazer with his HLI badge, so maybe he looked official and the ships' staff thought it was reserved for us.

Yarrow built warships for the navy: Type 21, 22 and 23 Frigates. Quite a few of them were launched while I worked there:

HMS Montrose,	HMS Campbeltown,
HMS Brilliant,	HMS Broadsword,
HMS Cornwall,	HMS Cottesmore,
HMS Battleaxe,	HMS Iron Duke,
HMS Coventry,	HMS Monmouth,
HMS Middleton,	HMS Brazen,
HMS Boxer,	HMS Cumberland,
HMS Beaver,	

One of the engineers told me that the names Battleaxe, Boxer, Broadsword and Brazen reminded him of his mother-in law.

It's quite an experience to watch a ship being launched, especially when you have seen its progress from laying the keel to being gradually transformed into a massive ship. After the launching ceremony, it moves slowly down the slipway and crashes into the water dragging the huge chains which stabilise it. There's complete silence until the ship safely hits the water and then the yard erupts. The workers cheer, whistle, throw their hats in the air, the brass band plays and some of the men are near to tears as another great Scottish achievement has been completed.

The pomp and pageantry is all part of a launch but in my opinion it is the ordinary workers, who made it possible, who should be on the official platform and perhaps the wee man who hit the first rivet should launch it. Some of the ships were launched by the Queen, Princess Margaret and Princess Diana. On the day of the launch, we office girls would go down to the dockside, watch the dignitaries arrive and then criticize their outfits. Prince Andrew served on HMS Brazen during the Falklands war.

The test engineers for whom I worked were real gentlemen, and always treated me with respect (even their pin-up calendars were taken down). They very rarely swore in front of me. As in all industries, there were the usual characters. Paul kept bees and sold the honey. He also made up a concoction of different blends of honey, filled small jars with it, and sold it at Christmas time as a hangover cure. We called him 'Buzz'. He detested the Royal Family, was very politically minded, and supported the Scottish National Party, the Labour party and the Tory party, whichever one agreed with his opinions at the time. His teacup was 'boggin' as it was only washed once a year, when Alistair gave it a 'spring clean' at the Fair. (Honest!)

Alistair was a member of the Theatre Guild and was an actor on and off stage. When he was going on the sea trials he asked me to post a birthday card to his wife and to be careful to send it off in plenty of time, as he had drawn a diagram inside the card to show her where her present was hidden.

Bobby was an apprentice and liked to play tricks on people. He would sellotape the buttons down on the cradle of the telephone so that when it rang and I lifted the receiver the phone kept on ringing. One day he played a stupid joke on one of the typists. He got a fish's head (don't ask me why) from the canteen, put it in a brown envelope, and sent it to her anonymously through the internal post. The typist went completely hysterical, thought there was a contract out on her, and nearly called the police. Bobby had to own up and was summoned to the manager's office, where he was severely reprimanded. He was very lucky not to have been dismissed.

Roger fancied one of the girls who worked in the print room and used to give her a lift to the ferry after work. Then one night she opened the car door and knocked a cyclist down. He claimed on Roger's insurance and that was the end of a beautiful friendship! Joe was a fitness fanatic, cycled to work every day, and was always off with a cold. He was nicknamed 'Joe Ninety' because he wore huge specs like the character in 'Thunderbirds'.

Malky was always falling out with his wife. One day she phoned the office to speak to him only to find that he was on sea trials for three weeks and hadn't told her.

Gary was another apprentice and a bit 'dippy'. Being an apprentice, he had to keep notes on the work he had done during the week. On Friday he handed his notebook to Mr Fleming, who, after reading it, came storming out of the office and called him in. Gary had been working on the sewage system and instead of using the word 'waste' he had written sh★★★. One morning he was sitting at his desk and suddenly remembered that he should have been at his brother's wedding.

Andy was called 'harpic' because he was 'round the

bend'. Willie bought two 'meat' pies for his lunch, smothered them with brown sauce, and discovered they were apple. Dick was a teuchter who came from Jura and thought all grandmothers should sit in rocking chairs, wear shawls and spin wool! Tommy worked in the contracts department and had an obsession about being the first to sign the register in the morning. If anyone signed before him, he ripped the page out and started a new one. There was a Pakistan working on the ship, and one Sunday, as he couldn't manage to come in for overtime, he sent his brother instead. The foreman wasn't too pleased and asked whether he thought the ship was a bloody Packy shop! There was another wee man who worked in the contract department. As he was going bald, he covered the bald patches with black boot polish. (Honest!)

Gordon's hobby was cooking and he sold his home-made lasagna and wholemeal bread to the men in the office. Although he took part in the master chef competition on television, he didn't win.

Sandy was married, but still did all the cooking, cleaning, washing and ironing. He stopped work on Friday afternoon and if it was a dry sunny day he was 'ecstatic' because it meant that he would get the washing dried.

Charles lived on his own, came to work early, and washed his feet in the 'gents' wash hand basin. (Honest.) He went on holiday to Millport for a week and took travellers' cheques with him.

Phyllis, who worked in the print room, brought her telephone to work every day to prevent her daughter using it. She had phoned the chatlines and ran up a bill of £400.

Joanne was the only female electrician. Although she

was only five foot and a bit 'butch', she did her 'telegram girl' at birthday parties and wore black fishnet stockings, black basque and a top hat. She also went to jiving classes with 'Joe Ninety'.

'Ginny' Jenny, who worked in the purchasing department, went to the off licence at lunch time, bought a half bottle of gin, and when she came back, sat in the toilet cubicle, ate her sandwiches and drank the gin. (Honest)

Dougie was rather henpecked. Sometimes, without telling him, his wife would 'pop' into the travel agents and book a few days' holiday for herself, leaving him with the dog.

Although there was a good canteen in Yarrow's, some engineers didn't use it, and as we had a 'howff' on the landing with a small cooker, one of my 'unofficial' duties, if they were working all morning on the ship, was to put their pies, chicken or curries in the oven to be ready at lunchtime.

A sense of humour was essential. When wearing a black and white outfit I was a liquorice allsort; in a lemon dress I was a canary – some said a sunflower; and a blouse with spots made their eyes go funny.

On one occasion I was getting double glazing windows put in. A test form was left on my desk requesting three photocopies and signed C.R. Smith. As there was no one in our office called Smith, I thought it must be for the navy. After I had copied the form, I couldn't find any 'Smith' until I finally realised that it was a 'wind-up' as C.R. Smith was a double-glazing firm!

After I had been working in the quality assurance for nearly twelve years, staff cutbacks were introduced in the department, so I was 'surplus to requirements'.

Office colleagues at Yarrows'

Accordingly I was transferred to the Ship Support Group.

This was the Main Record Centre, where the confidential records of every single ship in the Royal Navy were stored. I still worked for the engineers and electricians, but instead of testing equipment on the ship, they were permanently in the office. This was because their work involved making alterations to the original drawings if any changes were made to the layout of the ships. The Ship Support Group was also a good crowd of men to work for, and my duties were similar to those I had been doing except that there was more involvement with microfilms, microfiche and the reprographic machine. The drawings were altered continuously because so many changes were having to be made due to the Wrens now serving on board.

After a while I taught myself word processing, which made my work a bit more interesting. I now did some typing for my boss, Mr Jamieson, who would call me into his office and spend hours talking about every detail of his very successful heart bypass operation. I was really glad that it was a success, but after a few years of 'repeats', I now feel qualified to do the operation myself! After four years in the Ship Support, more cutbacks were proposed, so this time I was made redundant. However, being near retiring age, I was quite pleased; I had been working for many years. Although I didn't miss the work, I did miss the company and the rapport and found it difficult to adjust to a different routine. However I decided to use the time and opportunity to write my 'memoirs'!

Part Three
Snow in Summer
And
High Noon

CHAPTER 8

Early Holidays in Scotland and Abroad

THE CHILDREN HAD GONE THEIR SEPARATE WAYS and Alex and I now planned a first holiday on our own, a 'bed-and-breakfast' holiday in the Highlands, travelling in the orange mini which we had by this time acquired. Our first stop was at Ullapool. Our hotel, which overlooked Loch Broom, turned out to be quite 'posh'. Although all the waitresses were wearing tartan uniforms, they were in fact Filippinos. For our breakfast we ordered bacon and eggs and the eggs turned out to be 'sunny side up'. As I don't like soft eggs, I asked Alex if he would like mine. He didn't really want it but I was so persistent that I leaned right over to put it on his plate. Then – splatt! It landed right in the middle of the sugar bowl, scattering the sugar all over the table. Alex was fuming and a sharp exit was made!

The next day we crossed by ferry from Kyle of Lochalsh to the Isle of Skye. Here I had my second disaster. We were sitting in a restaurant in Portree and I had left my bag on the floor beside me. The waitress tripped over the strap, dropped the tray which she was carrying, and spilt coffee all over the lovely white tablecloth. Another sharp exit!

My third 'error' occurred on the way to Pitlochry. I misread the road map and as a result we landed up in the middle of Rannoch Moor. Alex lost his temper, the air went blue and he threw the road map out of the car window. So if anyone has found a small leather book full of road maps on Rannoch Moor, it's mine!

After spending some time at Pitlochry, we decided to travel to Arisaig. Accordingly we booked 'a-bed-ahead' at the tourist centre so that we wouldn't have to look for accommodation when we arrived there. The tourist board gave us the booking form with the name of the house, 'Morar', where we were to stay, and off we went. We had bought a new map.

'Do you think you'll manage to follow the road map this time?' asked Alex sarcastically.

After we had been travelling for miles and miles we could still see no sign of Arisaig and by this time it was getting dark. Furthermore, we were in the middle of nowhere and running out of petrol. I was panicking and Alex was getting madder and madder.

'Are you sure you've read the map right?'

'Of course. There it is marked right there.'

The orange mini

'Let's see the booking form.'

'For Christ's sake, it's Arisaig we should be heading for, no' bloody Ardrishaig.'

You've guessed it! I hadn't just misread the map again but misspelt the name of the place. Arisaig was in the opposite direction and the air once again went blue. Eventually we found a garage which had one petrol pump and telephone box. Alex filled up with petrol and I phoned the people at 'Morar' to explain that we had got lost and wouldn't be staying after all! However, we did find a nice bed-and-breakfast place near Easdale and enjoyed the next few days.

Our best BB and evening meal was 'Dee Valley' in Ballater, which was owned by Evelyn and Sandy Gray. It was a very popular guest house with tourists, as it is situated between Braemar and Banchory and accessible for touring the Highlands. However, the main attraction was the hospitality of our hosts. Every visitor was equally welcomed, the meals were excellent and plentiful and the rooms spotlessly clean. Evelyn and Sandy were very helpful and advised their guests where the best places were to visit during their holiday.

Alex and I kept going back to 'Dee Valley' and for over twenty years have been great friends with Evelyn and Sandy. We spent many lovely holidays with them and we were invited each year to celebrate Hogmanay.

On New Year's eve there would be a concert or bothy night in the Victoria Hall. Just before midnight Evelyn would serve steak, onions and roast potatoes and after the bells we would all first foot nearly the whole of Ballater, sometimes wading through snow up to our knees. Then on New Year's Day, Sandy and Evelyn's friends came to 'Dee Valley' where we all had a terrific party.

Among the guests would be Sid and Annie, Tibby and Ernie, Myra and Theodore, Ivy and Paddy, Bill and Margaret and anyone else who came to first foot. Ernie had been a German P.O.W. during the war but had stayed on in Ballater, married Tibby and become the local plumber. Paddy works with the council, has served with the mountain rescue for nearly thirty years, and received the MBE from the Queen. Myra was a lovely singer. Theodore, her husband, was a story teller. He told us about his father who owned a butcher's shop and had put a collection box on the counter with a notice saying 'money for the blind'. His customers, thinking it was for a good cause, gave generously, but when the box was full he promptly bought a blind for the shop window!

As we usually left the following day, Alex had to limit his intake of spirits, so he was delegated to be the 'waiter' and serve the food and drinks. There was always a huge variety of food to choose from, including venison, salmon, home-made cakes, sweets and sandwiches with various fillings. On one occasion Alex and Sandy brought in a huge salmon and handed it round for everyone to take a piece. When they came to Evelyn she whispered, 'that's oor bloody denner for the morn.' She had only left the salmon in the kitchen to cool.

Once when Evelyn was about to go to the bingo, their chimney caught fire. However, after a few attempts, Sandy managed to get it under control so off she went. The minute she walked into the hall a loud cheer went up. You see, being a close community, everyone had known that the chimney was on fire and as most of the members of the fire brigade were bingo callers, the game couldn't start until Evelyn appeared in case they were called out!

The Royal Family were on holiday at Balmoral Castle and as they always attend Crathie Church on a Sunday, Alex and I decided we would go and see them. We set off in our mini and travelled along the South Dee road towards Balmoral and Crathie. We knew there would be security police in the area but when we approached the castle there were none in sight, so we carried on towards the church.

As we turned the corner, right in front of us were hundreds of people lining both sides of the bridge we were to cross. They were waving and looking inside our car and then they all started to cheer. We didn't know what was happening until we looked behind and saw the royal car following us with the Queen and Prince Philip. Suddenly there was panic everywhere as the police realised that the little orange Mini shouldn't have been there, and they frantically waved us off the bridge and into the car park. After Alex had assured them that we were not assassins, they let us go!

Over the years we had been to most holiday places in Scotland, England and Wales, so we now thought about venturing abroad. We decided on a coach tour, so we booked with Cotters and our first trip abroad was to Küssnacht in Switzerland. We travelled to Birmingham for an overnight stay and after breakfast to Dover. From there we crossed by ferry to Calais through Belgium and into Switzerland. Our hotel, 'Seehof', overlooked Lake Lucerne and a few nights after we arrived, the courier arranged a folk evening for our bus party at the casino.

It was a glorious evening and we sailed by motor launch across the lake and up to the jetty which led straight into the casino. Alex had on a white dinner jacket and black bow tie and thought he was James

Bond! I had on a long evening dress and I thought I was Miss Moneypenny. Our tickets included entry to the folklore evening, two free drinks and, as an extra treat, we could also use our tickets for entry to the casino's gambling tables or to the strip club. Needless to say, with all the wives there, it had to be the gambling!

The folklore entertainment was held in a huge theatre above the casino and there were hundreds of coach parties from various countries. During the evening the hosts asked for couples of different nationalities to come on stage and take part in some of the fun, so Alex and I were nominated to represent Scotland. On stage we both took part in the traditional Swiss dancing, singing and yodelling.

Alex also tried his skill at blowing one of the long Alpine horns. Later in the evening we went to the casino and placed a bet of four Swiss francs on the roulette table. We won eight back, so we took it and left while our luck was still in!

The following day we went on a trip to Mount Titlis, which was 10,000 feet high. The only way to reach the summit was by funicular railway and cable car. At first I refused point blank to go as I was scared of heights, but as Alex wouldn't go and leave me at the bottom, I reluctantly agreed. The funicular railway went up the mountainside practically vertically. When it finally stopped at the cable car station, everyone got off and we all clambered into the car, including the skiers and their skies, leaving hardly any room to move. By this time I was terrified. The cable car then swung out and seemed to hang in mid air for ages before making its way up the mountain.

I was so relieved when it stopped – until I realised that we would have to travel on two more cable cars before reaching the top. By this time I was completely numb! 'Now listen, everybody,' said the courier, 'when you get to the top of the mountain, don't run around too energetically as the air up here is thin and might affect your breathing.' That was it! I stopped breathing on the spot, and when we did reach the top I practically crawled out of the cable car. On top of the mountain, although there was deep snow all around, the sun was very hot and some people were skiing while other were sun bathing in deck chairs. There was an ice palace, souvenir shop and a restaurant where we could eat our packed lunch. We always had hard-boiled eggs in our package, and from being scared in the cable car, I must have gripped my packed lunch so tightly that my egg

By cable car up Mount Titlis

was crushed to bits. I was never so glad to reach flat ground again.

When we arrived back at the hotel my friends gave me a postcard with a picture of the cable car which they had signed, just to prove that I had reached the top of Mount Titlis. On our journey home from Switzerland we stopped at Montreux for lunch.

The menu was written in French and when we ordered what we believed was chicken, it actually turned out to be frogs' legs! We had already eaten them when the waiter asked if we had eaten frogs' legs before, as we seemed to have enjoyed our lunch! We travelled home again via the Somme Valley and Vimy Ridge to Calais.

Next year we went back to Switzerland but this time to Interlaken, staying at the Royal St George Hotel. From here we visited Zurich and the old town of Berne. In Berne there was a deep bear pit where black bears are kept in captivity. Legend has it that if ever the bears disappear, so will Berne. We went to the Grindelwald to see the Trumbelbeck Falls, which are the biggest in Europe, and then to Donauschingen where the River Danube starts. It wasn't really blue, as the song suggests, but rather dullish grey. The next day we went to the fish hatcheries at Blasue and in the evening to a night club, where the singer was very good and where we danced all night.

Switzerland is a beautiful country with spectacular scenery, spotlessly clean, famous for cuckoo clocks and cow bells. All the cows wear bells around their necks and can be heard for miles. The bigger the bell, the more prized the cow is, and some of the bells seemed so big that the cows could hardly walk! The houses look like chocolate boxes. They are covered with baskets of flowers and make the countryside highly colourful. All of the houses fly the Swiss Flag.

Austria was our next venture and Seefeld was our base resort. From here we visited Innsbruck and Salzburg. Innsbruck, which is the capital of the Austrian Tyrol, has long narrow streets, lots of shops and market stalls, and is surrounded by mountains. It is a very popular town with tourists, and one of the attractions is the building with the solid gold roof built by Maximilian, son of Francis Charles, Archduke of Austria. He became Emperor of Mexico in 1832. Innsbruck hosted the 1984 Olympic games and the original Olympic-size ski jump built for the games is still there.

Salzburg was a much larger town with beautiful parks and buildings. This is where Mozart was born and the 'Sound of Music' was filmed. Inside Mozart's house, in the music room, were some of his manuscripts and other historical mementos. From there we went to the location where 'Sound of Music' was filmed and on the way the courier showed us the house where the real Von Trapp family had lived. It was nothing like the mansion used in the film but looked like a secluded castle high up on the mountainside. We stopped at the summer house where they filmed the song-and-dance sequence for 'you are sixteen going on seventeen' and I couldn't resist dancing round the benches and singing the song. We also saw the churchyard where the family hid from the Germans and the monastery, where I think one of the Von Trapp boys is now a monk.

There was another trip to Oberammergau, which is in Bavaria. Here the 'Passion Play' is performed in an outdoor theatre by the local residents every ten years. This play is performed by the villagers to show their devotion and thanksgiving for a miracle which ended

A painted house at Oberammergau

the black death. It was rife in the village many years ago. The village nestles in the Ammer valley surrounded by the Bavarian mountains, quite isolated but very attractive, as all the houses are beautifully painted on the outside with various scenes. So many tourists visit Oberammergau that it's rather commercialised and there are lots of woodcraft shops. On our way back to Seefeld we passed various Bavarian castles, including 'Mad Ludovic's', on which the castle in Walt Disney's Snow White was modelled. We stopped at Berchtesgarten where we saw Hitler's retreat, 'The Eagles Nest', which was high up in the Bavarian mountains. The only way to reach it was by cable car.

En route to our holiday resorts, the coach tours stopped at various places for overnight stays or simply to enable the passengers to spend a few hours sightseeing. One overnight stay was at Dijon in France. In the evening Betty, Elizabeth, Jack, Ian, Alex and I decided to go into town. The men had left before us and when we caught up with them they were on the opposite side of the street.

We wolf-whistled at them and for fun Betty flashed the edge of her petticoat. We didn't notice a pub across the road where the men drinking were staring at us. As they couldn't see our men at the other side, they must have thought we were trying to pick them up. In a panic we dashed across to joined Alex, Ian and Jack and when we walked past the pub with them, the men were standing at the door with big grins on their faces thinking these must be our 'pick ups'. The next day, after travelling through the Black Forest in Germany, we stopped at Boppard for a short cruise down the Rhine. It was a beautiful sail. On one side of the river were forbidding looking castles and on the other beautiful vineyards. We sailed past the dangerous Lorelei rock, where in days gone by there had been many shipwrecks. Legend has it that once upon a time a mermaid sat on the rock and lured the sailors to steer their ship towards it to make them strike it and sink.

Another place where we enjoyed an overnight stay was Aalter in Belgium. We were at the Hotel Capitole, which had a cinema, a beautiful dining room with mirrors round the walls, and a decorated ceiling with huge crystal chandeliers. Our bedroom, however, wasn't so attractive. There was a huge old-fashioned wooden four-poster bed with grotesque gorgon figures carved on the bedposts and weird looking birds carved on the furniture. The bed sagged in the middle. We finished up on the floor and then stayed awake the whole night in case Dracula appeared!

That evening we had soup for dinner and seeing what I thought were croutons on the table, I scattered some on my soup. Instead of floating on top, however, they started to swell; the soup disappeared and I was left with a plate of saps! Alex wasn't at all pleased, 'For Christ's sake hurry up and eat the bloody stuff before someone sees you.' Anyway Alex didn't manage to eat his own soup either. The man across the table from us took out his false teeth to eat and it put him right off!

Paris, via Fountainbleu Palace, was our next stopover and we stayed at 'Club Mediterranéan', which was a luxurious hotel on the 'Victor Hugo' boulevard.

On our arrival we found that the hotel which had originally been booked for us, the Penta, was still being occupied by American tourists. A strike was in progress at the airport and they had refused to vacate their rooms until it was over. Our compensation was to find ourselves staying at one of the most expensive hotels in Paris. That evening we were taken on a sail down the River Seine. We passed Notre Dame Cathedral, the Statue of Liberty (It is the original one; the American one is a larger version presented by France) and passed under a number of the bridges of 'Paree', which were beautifully illuminated. Afterwards the driver took us on a tour. We saw the Champs Elysées, the Arc de Triomphe, the Eiffel Tower and the famous Lido Club. Here the cabaret consisted of topless dancers and champagne cost (at that time!) fifty-five pounds a bottle. Nancy, who was on our tour, didn't like the French, so she spent the entire time in the hotel.

From Paris we travelled to Heidelberg, which has the oldest university in Germany, associated with the 'Student Prince'. Our hotel, the 'Park', overlooked the River Neckar.

On our return we had our first experience of going through the customs at Dover.

'Right, Ellen,' said Alex, 'we're going through customs, so don't panic because they might think we've got something to declare.'

'But we haven't got anything to declare.'

'I know, but if they see you're panicking they might search us.'

'But it doesn't matter if we are searched. We don't have anything!'

'Just don't panic.'

'Right, sir,' said the customs officer, 'anything to declare?'

Silence!

The officer then searched our cases and my handbag and of course, as he didn't find any 'contraband', he waved us through.

'That was close,' said Alex.

'What do you mean close. We didn't have anything!'

'I know but we might've had.'

(Was it me or was it him?)

We were the only ones to be searched. 'Mrs Thanks Awfully' got through with a valuable painting, wee Jeannie with cigarettes up her jumper, and Nellie with whisky down her knickers. And I was the one told not to panic! We secretly called one lady 'Mrs Thanks Awfully', as this was her favourite saying whenever anybody helped her. Before the end of the holiday she fell and broke her arm. She had to go home with a 'stookie'.

'That was a lovely hotel we were in,' said Bob, 'there was even a tiny baby bath in the bathroom.'

The 'tiny baby bath' was actually the bidet!

Bob was a bachelor travelling on his own and he became friendly with Janet, who was also unmarried. Their rooms were on the same floor and she was having trouble with the shower, so with only her dressing gown on, she knocked on Bob's door to ask him to fix it. As Bob was just about to have his shower, he answered the door with only a towel wrapped around him, but agreed to help. But when they attempted to go into Janet's room the door was locked. Suddenly Bob's door blew shut too and they were left stranded in the corridor. We were all in hysterics because Janet came from Edinburgh and was a right 'toffynose'.

We had made numerous friends during our bus tours and eight of us stayed friends for many years. Betty and Jack Forgie and their daughter Elizabeth from Clydebank, Ian Balfour from Bishopbriggs, and Margaret and Philip Clifton who came from Preston in Lancashire and met up with us at our various resorts.

When travelling by coach the journeys could be quite long and boring so to pass the time we would have a sing-song or the courier would play music tapes.

'Hiv' ye got ony Sidney Devine tapes?' shouted wee Jeannie.

'Who's Sidney Devine?' asked Oliver (the courier), who was of course English.

Suddenly for his benefit, there was a chorus of: 'Tiny bubbles in the wine, make me happy, make me feel fi-i-i-ne.'

'Sorry,' said Oliver, 'I've never heard of him.'

'Bloody sassanach!' muttered somebody.

However, at our next coffee stop the courier bought a Sidney Devine tape!

Now it just so happened that I had my Sidney Devine tee shirt with me, which I had bought at one of his concerts. It had 'Sidney Devine Country' written on it. The next day, on our coach trip to Innsbruck, the 'Devine' tape was duly played and as Sidney was belting out the 'Crystal Chandelier', I whipped off my jacket and paraded up and down the bus passage showing off my tee shirt. I received a standing ovation and had made wee Jeannie's day!

Elizabeth, Ian, Alex and I had bought 'gazzoos' and as we were travelling through Germany, much to the amusement of the other passengers, we started to play on our 'gazzoos', 'Colonel Bogie' and 'Hang out your Washing on the Siegfried Line'. Betty accompanied us on the paper and comb. It was hilarious!

As usual on some coach tours, we had to endure the 'single' female who flirts with everyone's husband. One evening after dinner we were all sitting round the table when our particular example of the breed came over and asked Alex if he could fix her camera, which had jammed.

While he was fixing the camera she stood behind him and began to massage his shoulders and run her fingers through his hair and of course he was lapping this up. There was a bowl of fruit on the table so I took one of the peaches and threw it at her but it hit Alex instead. Everyone at the table was stunned. Alex was fuming, went into a huff for two days, and made me wish it had been a tin of peaches!

After a few years of bus tours, Betty suggested that perhaps we should travel abroad by plane as it would be much quicker. The very thought of flying terrified me, so Alex and I opted to travel overland and meet them at Westendorf in Austria. However, the journey we chose turned out a bloody nightmare!

We travelled by the overnight sleeper from Glasgow to London and when we arrived at London we found complete chaos everywhere as this was the week Prince Charles and Diana were getting married. Scaffolding was being put up all over the city for vantage points and the place was teeming with tourists. We had to spend most of the day in London until it was time to catch our connecting train to Dover, where we then crossed the Channel by hydrofoil. It skimmed over the water so fast that it did the journey in four minutes flat! We then boarded our continental coach for an overnight journey to Austria. Our seats were at the front of the coach. There was no leg room and we had to sit with our knees practically touching our chins. The whole journey took nearly two days and when we finally arrived at Westendorf it was bloody snowing. The snow lasted for three days but after that it became really warm and the sun shone continuously for the rest of our holiday.

A beer festival was being held in Westendorf and the whole village was cordoned off to make it traffic free. Hundreds of people came and it lasted non-stop for two days. There was beer by the gallon, barbecued chicken to the accompaniment of folk dancing and singing. After each song was finished, the locals stood up, raised their glasses and shouted 'Prosit'. We raised ours and shouted 'Roast Pork'!

The courier had arranged ten pin bowling competitions at one of the neighbouring hotels. Alex was appointed 'captain' but the first evening we were having a 'carry on'. As a result, our team lost and we were given the booby prize, a large glass boot filled with beer from which we all had to drink. However, on the following evening Alex donned his Scotland top, we got down to really serious business, and we won the competition. There was an English woman in our team and as we didn't know her name, we called her Vera Lynn. I don't know if she could sing, but she certainly didn't know much about ten pin bowling as she showed when she said: 'Excuse me, captain, what position do I play?'

When anyone hit a 'strike', they received a small glass of schnapps and had to stand on a chair to drink it. I gained three strikes, was voted the best bowler of the evening, and so I had four schnapps! For winning the competition our team received a bottle of champagne but I didn't have any as I was feeling rather woozy. On our way home a small Austrian boy spotted Alex's Scotland top and shouted, 'Ah, Kenny Dalgleish!'

The next evening in the café we all decided to have a glass of milk. While drinking the milk and having a great laugh as usual, one of the holiday makers came over and asked us what the white stuff was that we were drinking. Looking confused, we replied that it was milk. 'Oh,' she said, 'I thought as you were enjoying yourselves so much, it must be some special Austrian drink made by the locals.'

From Westendorf we went on a coach trip up the Gross Glockner mountain. Once again this was, for me, a rather scary experience as it was thousands of feet to the top and there were twenty-six hairpin bends which the driver had to negotiate. Although it was a scorching hot day when we left, the further we travelled up the mountain the more the weather changed until we became engulfed in snow. Halfway up the driver stopped to let us have a snowball fight but when we finally reached the top we couldn't see a thing for mist and snow and it was freezing. The Gross Glockner is the venue for the yearly 'Milk Cycle Race' and it must be very gruelling for the cyclists.

The usual 'folklore' evening was held at the hotel. The Austrian men wear their 'lederhosen', which are short leather trousers with braces, and perform the traditional thigh-slapping dance. Alex and a few of the men rolled up their trousers, put on one of the dancers' jackets and joined in the fun. After dark, to commemorate the birth of Mozart, skiers staged a torchlight procession down the mountain ski slopes.

We went on another trip by local bus to Kitzbuhl and Kitzberg and on the way home, when the bus became full, instead of some of the passengers standing, they sat on somebody's knee, no matter who they were.

Before even packing a pair of socks, the first thing to go into the case was the continental teamaker, teabags, sugar, powdered milk and biscuits. (Betty always made a large fruit cake to take with us). Whoever had the biggest room in the hotel, that was the one where we would all congregate at supper time. It was usually Betty and Jack's as they had a family room. At one hotel, after collecting their keys in order to let Ian know which room they were in, Elizabeth held up the key and shouted: 'Ian I'm in room forty-eight!' The look on the passengers' faces was priceless for Ian was a bachelor and, being on his own, had a separate room. Elizabeth was always appointed our own personal 'courier' and was in charge of the 'kitty'.

Austria is such a beautiful country. It always looks as if the countryside has been 'spring cleaned' before the tourists arrive. The houses are mostly wooden chalets. They are decorated with masses of flowers and fly their national flag.

CHAPTER 9

Further Tours in Europe

SORRENTO IN ITALY WAS OUR NEXT HOLIDAY but this time I was persuaded to fly! For months before our holiday I was a nervous wreck at the mere thought of flying and the minute I stepped on the plane I wanted to get back off again. I felt so claustrophobic that I actually began to panic, but eventually my friends calmed me down before the plane took off.

After a while, just as I was just starting to relax, the pilot welcomed everyone on board and proceeded to tell us that we were now flying at 31,000 feet and 350 miles per hour. Instant panic! I was gradually calming down again when the pilot suddenly announced, to my great relief, that in twenty minutes we would be arriving at Naples airport. I had done it!

Our hotel, the 'Flora', was brilliant. On the roof there was an outdoor swimming pool and the balcony over-looked the Bay of Naples and Mount Vesuvius. As it is extremely hot in Italy, it is the custom to have a siesta in the afternoon, which we enjoyed. After dinner we would spend the evening at the outdoor cafés, drinking cold beer or cappuccino and watching the world go by. This was the first time I had ever worn a bikini so naturally wanted a photograph taken. As I was rather self-conscious about wearing one, I would rush up to the swimming pool before anybody else had arrived. Alex would then take the photos and I would rush back again. When the spool was being removed from the camera, it seemed to spin, and we thought that some of the photos wouldn't come out, so I went through the whole procedure again. When they were developed all the photos were perfect, so that I now have nearly two spools of bikini photos. The developer must have thought that I was bloody vain! Near the hotel was a café with a sign outside which read: 'Lady

In the swimming pool at Sorrento

Di makes a lovely cappuccino and a nice teapot'. I think the owner was trying to impress the tourists. This was also the year Italy had won the world cup. There was a great festival atmosphere and flags were flying from every building. Italians are very friendly and romantic, but there are lots of gigolos too.

Being tourists, eight of us decided to break the custom of afternoon siesta and go for a cruise along the Bay of Naples to the Moorish village of Ischia, where we stopped for lunch. We all ordered pizza with chips and when the waiter came with our order, instead of bringing eight portions, he had brought eight whole pizzas the size of dinner plates and a huge bowl of chips. We could have fed all the passengers and the crew. On the way back we sailed to the Isle of Capri where the legendary Gracie Fields and her Italian husband used to live.

Another day Ian, Elizabeth, Alex and I decided to travel by train along the coast to Pompeii. We thought it would be a nice picturesque journey but the train went straight through the mountain, travelled at about a hundred miles an hour, the only time we saw the sea was when it stopped at the station, and when we finally arrived at Pompeii the guides had decided to go on strike. We didn't know why, but seemingly in Italy these lightning strikes happen all the time and the causes may be quite trivial. Next we had to hang around for ages in the tremendous heat, which must have been about one hundred degrees (in the shade), and I have to admit Noel Coward was right. Only mad dogs and Englishmen go out in the midday sun! After about two hours and two litres of cold drinks, which they sold outside the gates, we were finally allowed inside.

Pompeii was the town which was caught unawares

in A.D. 78 by an avalanche of volcanic dust from the erupting Vesuvius. The whole village and population were completely buried by the dust. Many centuries later it was excavated and everything and everyone was found exactly as they had been when the tragedy happened. The shops with all the utensils still on the shelves are intact, and wonderful paintings on the walls of the houses are still visible. Also in a few of the houses are the bodies of people still encased in the lava. A small dog tied to a post is encased in the same way. Along the streets are deep grooves which were made by the Roman chariots and part of the outdoor Amphitheatre is still standing. Being in Pompeii struck us as quite an eerie experience; you could practically re-live the tragedy.

The next day we took the local bus to Amalfi and, as Elizabeth and Ian had been on this journey before, they told me to take the window seat and enjoy the exhilarating view. We started off along the country roads, passed the olive groves and on towards the coast, where the road we were to take was built on the outside of the cliffs. As we climbed higher and higher, the ships on the water below dwindled to the size of the models found in cornflake packets, while a private plane was flying along the side of the cliffs directly underneath us and we were looking out on a sheer drop to the sea.

Every time the bus turned a corner the two back wheels seemed to be hanging over the cliff, the driver kept sounding the horn continuously to warn oncoming traffic that we were approaching, we crossed a narrow bridge which spanned the sea and there was a sheer drop on either side. By this time I was petrified and to the astonishment of the other passengers I sat on the floor of the bus until we arrived at Amalfi. Alex too

Myself in front of the Vatican

was a whiter shade of pale! Although Amalfi was a beautiful town with a lovely cathedral, I couldn't enjoy myself for thinking about the journey back.

A few days after I had recovered from my 'ordeal', Margaret, Philip, Alex and I went on a sight-seeing trip to Rome. We visited the ruins where the Colosseum once stood and where the gladiators (not the television ones!) fought to the death, just to amuse the Romans. We saw the Forum where Julius Caesar held court and the remains of the vast Amphitheatre. This has a dome with an opening at the top, but it is immensely high and built in such a way that when the rain comes in, it dries up before reaching the ground. We had lunch by the Fountain of Trevi, threw lots of coins into the fountain, made a wish, and then went to visit the Vatican, which was absolutely wonderful and awe-inspiring. There were statues of the twelve apostles surrounding the perimeter of the roof and St Peter's Square is really vast. Inside the Vatican are huge marble pillars, beautiful paintings and statues, many of them works of Michelangelo. We also visited the Sistine Chapel, where we saw the ceiling which he had painted in the sixteenth century. The Borgia apartments and Raphael's rooms are also in the Vatican, but they were closed at that particular time. Anyone, irrespective of denomination, should visit the Vatican if only for historic reasons. As she was a Catholic, Margaret wanted to know where the Pope was. We told her that he was probably in his air-conditioned room watching us and thinking: 'Bloody stupid tourists, walking about in the bloody heat! They must be mad!'

Margaret just laughed, but before we left she had an opportunity to attend a short Mass in one of the small chapels within the Vatican, so she was quite happy. The Vatican is separate from Rome and became a state city in 1929. It has its own broadcasting station, postage stamps, coinage, flags, etc; and the Swiss guards, who wear striking red uniforms, protect the palace at all times. On our way home we stopped at the Spanish

Steps. Back on the coach, our Italian driver was playing a tape of Pavarotti singing 'O solé mio'. We all joined in and sang 'just one cornetto', which has the same tune.

Each evening over the bay of Naples there were gorgeous sunsets. Alex wanted to photograph them but kept forgetting to bring his camera along and by the time he rushed back to our hotel room to get it, the sun would have completely vanished. This happened every evening and when we arrived home from holiday, someone had sent a postcard from Sorrento with a picture of a sunset. Written on the back of the card was, 'The sunsets are beautiful in Sorrento'. As in all hot countries, insects can be a nuisance and Italy was no exception. Ants were the biggest pests and they seemed to plague the hotel bedrooms. Betty and Jack's room seemed to be the worst, probably because of the supper goodies, including the sugar, being kept there. Betty used so much insect repellent, we practically had to wear masks in case we were killed off before the ants! Alex and I were the only ones who didn't have any ants in the room or on the veranda. We had brought some strong carbolic soap with us, as it's a great antiseptic, and we think the powerful smell kept them at bay.

On our next trip to Italy we chose Catolica, which is on the Adriatic coast. As we were travelling on a night flight, it entailed an early morning arrival at Rimini airport and then an hour's drive by coach to our hotel. After a few hours' rest before unpacking, we all decided to have a coffee and then a stroll along the promenade.

As we walked towards the beach, nearly every person we met was practically naked except for bikini bottoms or 'G' strings. As we were fully clothed, they kept staring at us and must have thought we were 'Mormons' or maybe 'morons'. I never felt so embarrassed at having clothes on! After a few days, however, we got used to seeing everyone topless, and with the heat being so intense, almost joined them but not quite. From Catolica we went on an excursion to San Marino, which is situated on a high plateau and is completely surrounded by Italy. As it is a Republic, before passing the checkpoint we handed over our passports to be stamped and then collected them on the way back. The policemen wear white uniforms, white gloves and white pith helmets. There were plenty of duty-free shops, where wine and spirits were very cheap, and every shop gave small samples to the tourists. There were a few tipsy passengers on the bus home.

The next day we travelled by coach to Venice and as it was very expensive to hire a gondola, we toured the city by water bus and afterwards we had our packed lunch in St Mark's Square. Here there were lots of pigeons, market stalls and an orchestra playing continuously. We walked across the 'Bridge of Sighs' where prisoners crossed on their way to be executed. We also visited San Marco church and the factory where beautiful Venetian glass is made. Everything in Venice was very expensive, even cold drinks and coffee. It was an exceptionally hot day and Alex was feeling unwell, so to cool down he waded into the canal and stood with the water almost up to his waist. The gondoliers were rowing past him and must have thought: 'Here's another bloody mad tourist'. Although Venice is crumbling and smells a little 'stale' we didn't really notice. It was so magical to be there.

Our flight home from Catolica was not until two

In Venice

o'clock in the morning, so to pass the time we all decided to go by local bus to Riccioni.

We enjoyed our evening there but while waiting for the bus back to the hotel, I remarked to Alex that we were in the wrong queue for Catolica. As usual he disagreed with me, but after about five minutes on the bus Elizabeth shouted, 'Alex, we're on the wrong bus!'

Now in Italy it doesn't matter how large the queue is, everyone is allowed on the bus. They are packed in like sardines and we were right in the middle! Panic set in and Jack kept ringing the bell for the driver to stop. He, however, ignored us until the next stop, where more people were embarking. By this time I was so claustrophobic that I could hardly breathe, and in getting off the bus I felled about a dozen passengers who were trying to get on! In the struggle to get off, Betty left a wee man wrapped round a pole and Ian had his wallet stolen. Luckily there were only ten pounds in it. I suffered so much nervous exhaustion that the flight home didn't bother me.

The following year we went to Mayrhofen, which is one of the prettiest villages in Austria. Although we had been in Austria before this time, we now visited fresh places. On our first excursion we travelled through the Brenner Pass, over the Europa Bridge and across the Austrian/Italian border to the small town of Vipiteno, which is very popular with tourists as leather goods are sold at bargain prices. There were lots of shops, cafés, street vendors and market stalls, all selling leather products. I bought some leather belts, handbags and purses for presents, Alex bought three cheap camera spools from a street vendor and when the photos were developed they turned out orange. Another time we travelled on an old-fashioned steam train to one of the mountain villages where, we were told, the Christmas carol 'Silent Night' had been composed. We chose the seats which were near the open window as we thought the view would be spectacular, but once the train had speeded up, smoke and cinders came flying in and the window wouldn't shut. Then when we arrived at our station and the train had left, we found ourselves in a deserted village miles from anywhere and the train wasn't due back for four hours.

There was no sign of the church where 'Silent Night' was allegedly composed; it was only the village that was 'silent'. We could find only one shop, where we bought some cool drinks, and as there was nothing of any interest, we waited at the station for the train to return. The village looked like a scene from a wild west movie, with nothing but miles of railway tracks disappearing into the distance, so that when the train finally came puffing over the horizon, we all started to sing 'High Noon'.

In the evening we took the local bus to the small village of Hintertux, where we were nearly eaten alive by enormous horse flies. I think this must have been the village where the thigh-slapping dance originated! The next day was a scorcher, so Alex and Jack decided to travel to the top of the mountain by cable car, which might be cooler, and then do a bit of exploring. It wasn't much cooler at the top but there was a café and bar, so after Jack had had a beer, he decided to sit in the sun and wait for Alex to come back from his walk. Jack fell asleep and got severe sunburn on his arms and legs, but when they returned home Jack didn't receive an ounce of sympathy from Betty, but only a row for being so damn lazy and not getting enough exercise.

The next evening we all went on a horse-and-carriage

ride around the village of Mayrhofen, and as there were eight of us and not all slimline, the horse was straining at the collar. We stopped at one of the hotels for refreshments, and when we left to ride home again the driver had changed the lovely leather carriage with one horse for a long wooden cart with two horses. The cart had straw on the floor and wooden seats along each side. As we trundled through the village, we must have looked like a reincarnation of the French revolution in which we were the aristocrats on their way to the guillotine. From our holiday resort it was a two-hour drive to the airport, and as we travelled along the motorway, the driver passed the turn off for Munich, where the airport was, and followed the sign for Berlin.

I could see the town of Munich in the distance getting further and further behind us, so true to my nature, began to panic. I thought we were all being hijacked to Berlin until the coach suddenly turned off the motorway right at the airport, where we were all body-searched – probably because I was still in a sweat and looked suspicious!

The following year Ian had suggested that we should all go to Kranjskagora in North Yugoslavia, but sadly he died suddenly of a heart attack in January. We were all devastated and thought of cancelling our booking. However, after much discussion we decided to go ahead as planned. Our 'Hotel Compas', which was situated at the foot of the mountains, had outdoor and indoor swimming pools. There was a night club in the basement and every evening a cabaret took place and the dancing lasted until the early morning. Once a week in the hotel a candle-lit dinner would be laid on, the cabaret singers would entertain us, and during the rest of the week at

Alex dancing

mealtimes there would be a keyboard player. On my birthday he played and sang happy birthday for me.

From Kranjskagora we travelled on a coach tour to Klangenfurt and the Julian Alps. There were some beautiful walks to be taken and on a few occasions we walked as far as the Austrian border. The chairlift was near our hotel, and I was persuaded by Alex and Jack to 'have a go' on it. As it didn't seem to be very high, I agreed. I was wrong! The chairlift went higher and higher and I became absolutely rigid with fear as I was dangling all alone in mid air with nothing on either side or underneath me but space. On reaching the next stop I jumped off while the chair was still moving. I refused to go on again, so after one of our usual 'friendly' arguments, Alex 'agreed' to walk back down the mountain with me and Jack took the chairlift. That evening we were to have attended a folk evening at another hotel, but there was a terrible thunderstorm and I 'declined'.

The following year our holiday resort was Opatija on the coast of Croatia (southern Yugoslavia). Our hotel, 'The Imperial', had once been used by royalty. It over-looked the Adriatic. From here we visited the riding school, where some of the famous Spanish Lipizzaner stallions were kept. In a huge indoor arena these magnificent horses performed their dance routines to music, and we were allowed to tour the stables where some of the Lipizzaners were bred.

On another occasion we attended an outdoor medie-val banquet arranged for us by our courier at one of the mountain villages. It was a beautiful evening as our coach set off to the village where the banquet was to be held. When we arrived, there were rows of long tables laden with food and wine and there was to be an open air medieval floor-show with traditional folk dancing. Suddenly, half way through the meal and entertainment, a terrific storm blew up with thunder, lightning and torrential rain. There was nowhere to shelter and as it was a very steep climb to the village, the buses were stationed at the bottom of the mountain. Thus we had a ten-minute walk downhill before we reached them. Everyone was drenched to the skin and as it was a one-hour drive from the village to our hotel, we had to remain soaked until we arrived there.

On our way home from Opatija, we left from Pula airport, which is very small. The customs point is a huge hangar. After going through the customs, our luggage was left on the tarmac. Everyone had to identify their cases before they were put on board. We seemed to be waiting for ages on the plane before take-off. At that point Betty suddenly said, 'Jack, that looks like our suitcase on the runway.' Sure enough, there was one solitary suitcase lying on the tarmac and it was theirs. Jack had forgotten to identify it and the authorities wouldn't allow the plane to leave until he did. On the flight I was just beginning to relax and enjoy my meal, when the plane hit an airpocket and dropped about a hundred feet. Ever since it has put me right off bloody flying (?).

Sadly, not long after our holiday in Yugoslavia, our friend Betty died. By this time our holidays with Margaret and Philip had tapered off, though we are still friends and keep in touch with them.

A few years later, Elizabeth, Jack, Alex and I went by Urquhart's coach tour to the Isle of Wight, where we stayed at a small family-owned hotel. We visited Osborne House, where Queen Victoria, Prince Albert and their children spent their summer holidays. It is a large house situated among acres of woodland, where we had a lovely picnic. Then we went into Osborne House, where Queen Victoria's possessions and many royal mementos are on display. We also visited a pearl factory, where Alex bought me a pearl necklace (at cost price) for my birthday. While we were there, the annual yachting race was held at Cowes and the royal yacht Brittania was in the harbour with Prince Philip and Prince Andrew on board. We booked a sail from Cowes to Southampton, where we did some shopping and visited a war museum. On the way back, our boat sailed past the royal yacht, but we didn't see any of the Royals. Every evening in the hotel there was either bingo, dancing or a cabaret.

Sadly, two years later Jack also died. Elizabeth has

now met Patrick and they are getting married. As her fiancé is of Irish origin, they spend most of their holidays in Ireland. We are still very good friends and are going to the wedding.

Alex and I booked a coach trip with Wallace Arnold and went to Ostend in Belgium, where our hotel was two minutes from the beach. It was a fishing port, so along the promenade there were rows of stalls selling all kinds of fresh fish, cockles, mussels, as well as that old faithful, fish and chips. From Ostend we went on a day trip to Amsterdam, where we visited a diamond factory. I regret to say that I was not given any diamonds because they weren't at cost price and it wasn't my birthday. Afterwards we took a boat trip along the canals, which turned out to be another bloody nightmare.

It was a scorching hot day. The boat was long and narrow and in addition to having glass windows, it was also equipped with a glass roof. As the sun beat down mercilessly, the boat became hotter and hotter. We had no shade whatever and, as we were sailing down the middle of the canal, there wasn't even a cool breeze from the water. It was an hour-long cruise, so we were nearly roasted alive!

On board, the guide sold ice-cold drinks, which helped a little. He also sold picture postcards of the interesting places we passed on the trip, so I bought twenty of them to send to my friends. The next day I went to buy stamps for them only to find that it was a local holiday in Ostend and that the post office was shut for three days. Newsagents only sold stamps if you bought their postcards, so I had to buy some more cards to send. Back in Scotland, I now have twenty postcards with views of Amsterdam!

From Ostend we went on a sightseeing tour of Brugge, visiting the British war graves at Passchendale, where Alex lost his brand new spectacles. On the way home we stopped at Manchester overnight, embarking for Glasgow the next day. The journey should have taken two hours, but what with picking passengers up here, dropping others off there, stopping for coffee breaks and changing buses, the driver took eight hours. Cotters' or Urquharts' tours were never like that. Every aspect of them was so well organised and such fun. When at last we arrived home we felt completely shattered and vowed never to go on a bus tour again!

In June 1995, we went to the wedding of Elizabeth and Patrick. It was a beautiful day, she was a lovely bride and we had a great time.